W9-CKS-944

MATERIALIST APPROACHES
TO THE BIBLE

716

I say that in my opinion you and Signor Galileo should act prudently by simply presenting things in a *hypothetical* rather than a categorical manner.

Letter of Cardinal Bellarmine to Father Foscarini (1615)
(Quoted by L. Geymonat, *Galilée*,
Paris: Laffont, 1968, page 128)

MATERIALIST APPROACHES TO THE BIBLE

Michel Clévenot

Translated by William J. Nottingham

ORBIS BOOKS

Maryknoll, New York 10545

The Catholic Foreign Mission Society of America (Maryknoll) recruits and trains people for overseas missionary service. Through Orbis Books Maryknoll aims to foster the international dialogue that is essential to mission. The books published, however, reflect the opinions of their authors and are not meant to represent the official position of the society.

Originally published as *Approches matérialistes de la Bible,* copyright © 1976 by Les Editions du Cerf, 29 boulevarde Latour-Maubourg, Paris

English translation copyright © 1985 by Orbis Books, Maryknoll, NY 10545

All rights reserved
Manufactured in the United States of America

Library of Congress Cataloging in Publication Data

Clévenot, Michel, 1932-
  Materialist approaches to the Bible.

  Translation of: Approches matérialistes de la Bible.
  1. Bible.   N.T.   Mark—Criticism, interpretation, etc.
2. Bible.   O.T.—Criticism, interpretation, etc.
I. Title.
BS2585.2.C5413   1985   220.6   84-14711
ISBN 0-88344-343-0 (pbk.)

Contents

Part II
THE GOSPEL ACCORDING TO ST. MARK,
OR A NARRATION OF THE PRACTICE OF JESUS

Translator's Foreword

It was not easy to settle on a title for this book because *Materialist Approaches to The Bible* seems to lend itself to misunderstandings. In English, "materialist" usually has an ethical connotation rather than a philosophical one. However, it was finally decided to use an exact translation of the author's title and thereby emphasize the terminology current in French theological discussions to which the book itself bears witness.

"Materialist" refers to the view of history and culture that Marxist social theory has popularized. It means that all consciousness is produced materially or by the material conditions in which people live, particularly by the kind of work they do and the social class to which they belong. In other words, a materialist approach does not allow for interpretations of life and experience from the standpoint of eternal truths or the will of God or abstract ideas working themselves out in daily life. The materialist approach means that a basic assumption about methods of historical understanding has been made, consisting of the attempt to discern how power is used overtly or subtly to dominate, brainwash, or exploit classes of people. So "materialist" has a technical meaning in this context and results essentially from a Marxist analysis of society.

However, the title is "Materialist Approaches"—in the plural. There are probably numerous readings of the Bible that could be made from a materialist standpoint, or at least many that would differ at one level or another, particularly as more or less data became known about various periods of biblical history. This is one that is sympathetic to the person of Jesus and to the prophetic movement to which he belongs. It is a materialist reading expressing Christian faith, a combination that is not at all incongruous in the light of the gospel this reading finds in the liberating practice of Jesus.

Materialist Approaches to the Bible has some important insights for the English-speaking world, particularly for North America. It might make the Bible important and interesting once again to a generation raised on sociology and a passion for justice. It might speak to that love for God that is left parched and arid by most experience in churches or that becomes trivialized in middle-class denominationalism. It might speak for the first time to Marxists of dimensions that the community of faith brings to a world of class struggle and new socialist societies. It might speak to those concerned about the deep changes required for a liberating revolution.

We might question some textual analysis of the author, such as the explanation of the open ending in the Gospel of Mark. Perhaps there was an original ending of one kind or another that has been lost. However, the implication for the practice of Christians who are extending the narration of the liberating practice of Jesus remains valid, as does the critique of the present ending of Mark, which was added by a later writer.

It is hoped that readers will find renewed appreciation for the Bible through this study and will be enabled to engage in the transformation of life through faith in the approachable Christ. That God achieves this by grace through the Holy Spirit is not a materialist consideration but stands as an indispensable point of reference for the theological criticism and resourcing of all our practice. It is part of the originality of Jesus' struggle against oppression and its insidious hypocrisy and for the liberation of men and women not only for a new society but for a new creation—a new kind of life in this redeemed world.

Preface to the English Translation

Since the publication in 1974 of the book by Fernando Belo, materialist readings of the Bible have had an astonishing success. [The English translation was published as *A Materialist Reading of the Gospel of Mark*, Trans. Matthew J. O'Connell (Maryknoll, N.Y.: Orbis Books, 1981).]

In November 1978 the theological journal *Lettre* organized in Paris an international conference of groups occupied with the materialist readings of the Bible; numerous delegations participated from all over Europe and from Quebec.

I am particularly happy that my book will be available to the English-speaking world, thanks to the translation of Bill Nottingham. In that respect, I would like to underline two points which seem to me to be very important: strictly speaking, there is no "method" of a materialist reading in the sense of a universally valid scientific system. What is scientific in our approaches is that, beginning with clearly defined hypotheses, we experiment, correct, and improve the procedures of our work. But what does seem to be established from now on is that materialist readings presuppose two things: (a) that we take as our point of departure the present struggles in which we are involved, so that we can reread the texts that have woven our history and free them from those who have used them to legitimize their own power; (b) that we take seriously the "materiality" of the text, which can be seen as the product of a practice of language (whose material is linguistic) situated in class struggles and within the dominant ideology of a given social structure. This means that language is considered to be an area of historical materialism, and that the reading of the text brings into play at the same time both language and history.

And since this book is published on American soil, I would like to dedicate it very modestly to Martin Luther King, Jr., and to Camilo Torres, who were led by the gospel to fight and die for justice and liberty. In the words of Walt Whitman, "To Thee, old cause!"

Foreword

Fernando Belo's *Lecture matérialiste de l'évangile de Marc* (Editions du Cerf, 1974) has raised a considerable echo. Translated into several languages and already in a second printing, it has been greeted as an important event by a great number of articles in France and abroad.

It proposes, in effect, a method and theoretical instruments that open up a radically new reading of the biblical texts. But the work is difficult, heavy, and complex. It takes courage and some preparation to follow it to the end.

As the one responsible for editing Belo's work, I thought it would be useful to present to the vast public, which this new access to the Bible interests, a smaller book, one that would be more modest and, I hope, more accessible.

To be sure, the pages that follow owe the best that is in them to the work of Belo, but they are not in any way a résumé or even an introduction. They offer simply some ways of approach for materialist readings of the Bible. The reader will not find here the complete study of all the biblical texts, of course, but certain perspectives that will permit a continuation of this research.

The chapters of part 1 were the result of a two-year seminar undertaken with some friends, including Fernando Belo himself. As for part 2, it was obviously inspired by the work of Belo, but in my own way and without engaging his responsibility.

To make the reading easier, the notes have been placed at the end of the book. One can look there to consult the sources from which I gathered my information.

Part I

The Bible or the Scriptures

Chapter 1

The Bible as Scripture

Today all those who want "to read the Bible" find themselves before an enormous book of hundreds of pages.

But the very title of the work—the Bible—tends to make the reader forget that it is a matter of *books*, a disparate collection of extremely different texts. It is a little like putting end to end under the same cover the *Song of Roland* (1150), the *History of Saint Louis* by Joinville (1309), the poems of Pierre de Ronsard (1550), some chapters of Montaigne (1580), a selection of laws from the time of Louis XIV and the Napoleonic Code, and finally the posters of May 1968 and an essay of Jean-Paul Sartre. This would be undoubtedly a relatively representative sample of France and of the French, but one might ask *who made this choice and why*? Of course, the biblical corpus was not put together that way, *a posteriori* and all at once! But those are precisely the questions that must be asked first of all, before beginning to read the Bible.

We have announced that our approach will be materialist. What does that mean?

In direct contrast to German philosophy [idealist]which descends from heaven to earth, here we ascend from earth to heaven. This is to say, we do not set out from what men say, imagine, conceive, nor from men as narrated, thought of, imagined, conceived, in order to arrive at men in the flesh. We set out from real, active men, and on the basis of their real life-process we demonstrate the development of the ideological reflexes and echoes of this life-process. [1]

3

This real activity of humanity, this practice, can be defined as "any process of *transformation* of a determinate given/raw material into a determinate *product*, a transformation effected by a determinate human labor."[2] Throughout this production process, men and women as the agents of production establish among themselves *social relationships of production*, that is, forms of ownership of the means of production, forms of distribution of products, and class structures. "The sum total of these relations of production constitutes the economic structure of society."[3] And "the economic structure of society always forms the real basis from which, in the 1st analysis, is to be explained the whole superstructure of legal and political institutions, as well as of the religious, philosophical, and other conceptions of each historical period."[4]

The *political* level thus concerns the institutions (the state and its apparatus of laws, army, schools, etc.) that regulate the places and roles of the agents of production.

The *ideological* level includes all the ideas or representations men and women derive from the mechanisms of production and all the attitudes or conduct that are a part of people's manner of living and are translations of those mechanisms. We must add that, in societies of classes, the dominant ideology is for the most part the ideology of the dominant class.[5]

We shall envisage, therefore, the texts that make up the Bible as *ideological products*. Our project will be to analyze the conditions in which they were produced. And our first step will be to set up, in a way, a historical table of contents of the different biblical texts.

BRIEF HISTORY OF THE BOOKS OF THE BIBLE

Around 1850 B.C. some groups of Semitic nomads appeared in Palestine (then called Canaan); nothing remains from this period except a few fragments such as the Song of the Well (Num. 21:17–18).[6]

Six centuries later, about 1250 B.C., a few Semitic tribes escaped (or were expelled)[7] from Egypt where they had been reduced to slavery. One group invaded Canaan from the south and became installed in the region of Beersheba and Hebron; another

THE DEVELOPMENT OF THE OLD TESTAMENT

Fragments of Old Traditions: Numbers 21:18 (Song of the Waterhole or Well)
Organization of Cycles of Traditions

NORTH
Cycle of Joseph:
Jacob, Israel, Moses, Ark of the Covenant, Sichem
Judges 5: Song of Deborah (Absence of Judah)
Exodus 21 and 23: Code of the Covenant of Horeb
Joshua 24: Covenant of Sichem
Judges 9 and 1 Samuel 8: Opposition to the Monarchy

SOUTH
Cycle of Judah:
Abraham, Isaac, Aaron, priesthood
Genesis 49: Blessing of Jacob (Judah favored)
Exodus 34: Code of the Covenant at Cades
1 Samuel 9: For the Monarchy

KINGDOM OF JUDAH AND ISRAEL (Jerusalem)
2 Samuel 9 to 20 and 1 Kings 1 and 2:
Yahwist Document (J)

KINGDOM OF ISRAEL (Samaria)
Prophetic Reaction: Elija, Elisha
1 Kings 17 to 2 Kings 13, Amos, Hosea
Elohist Document (E)
Deuteronomist Document (D)

KINGDOM OF JUDAH (Jerusalem)
Prophecies about the Kingdom: Isaiah 1 to 12
Scribes and Cantors: Proverbs, Psalms (18)
622 Discovery of Deuteronomy, reform of Josiah
Editing of the books of Joshua, Judges, Samuel,
and Kings
Deuteronomist prophecies of Jeremiah

587 Exile at Babylon. Role of the priesthood: The Priestly Document (P)
Ezechiel 40–48, Isaiah 40–55

583 The Return from Exile   Leviticus 1–7 (sacrifices) and 11–16 (purity)
Reconstruction of the Temple
Apocalyptic prophecies: Isaiah 24–27
Wisdom literature: Job

398 Esdras and Nehemiah impose the Law (Pentateuch: J plus E plus D plus P)
Revolt of the Maccabees. Book of Daniel (Apocalypse)
Qohelet (Ecclesiastes)

About 50. At Alexandria. Wisdom books.

JUDAISM

Year	Event
1850	Semites in Palestine
1700	Semites in Egypt
1250	The Exoduses
1200	Entrances into Palestine
1030	Saul
1000	David
970	Solomon
931	Split Between North and South
722	Capture of Samaria
587	Capture of Jerusalem
538	Edict of Cyrus
333	Alexander
142	Hasmoneans
63	Pompey

group crossed the Jordan and settled in the north around She-chem.[8] Little by little these tribes became sedentary, those of the north forming a kind of confederation with groups already there, a trace of which is to be found in the Covenant of Shechem (Josh. 24).

But in the eleventh century B.C., the Philistines occupied the country, which henceforth derived its name, Palestine, from them. Armed with iron weapons and chariots of war, they were invincible in open country. To resist them, the Semitic tribes gave themselves a king named Saul from the group in the north. In 1030 B.C. he was killed during the crushing battle and retreat in the plain of Jezreel at the foot of Mount Gilboa.[9] Then a man from the tribes of the South named David seized power. He suc-ceeded in having himself proclaimed first of all king of Judah (in the south) and then king of Judah and of Israel (in the North). He set up his capital in Jerusalem in 1000 B.C.

One of the sons of David named Solomon was his successor. At Solomon's court, about 950 B.C., someone edited *the first written text* of the Bible that comes to us in its entirety: the narration of the succession of David (2 Sam. 9–20 and 1 Kings 1 and 2).[10]

We shall study this fundamental text in more depth in the next chapter. But let us indicate here that to read it informs us about its own conditions of production and of those of the texts the exegetes call "the Yahwist document" (abbreviated J). It is nothing less than a royal edition of oral traditions of the tribes of the north and south, corresponding to the needs of Solomon's power.

Unfortunately, we no longer have this J document in its ori-ginal state in our modern editions. We shall see why in a moment. But the patient work of exegetes permits us to reconstruct it with a high degree of certainty. Recent editions of the Bible indicate in footnotes: "This part of the text comes from the Yahwist docu-ment."

To facilitate study, you will find here a complete list of "Yahwist" passages from the first two books of the Bible: Gene-sis and Exodus. If you have the patience, you will not be wasting your time if you mark these texts in your Bible; we suggest that you underline all the Yahwist passages in red. This will be useful to you for the reading which we are proposing.[11]

The Yahwist Document

Genesis: 2:4b–25; 3; 4; 5:29; 6:1–8; 7:1–5, 7–10, 12, 16b–17, 22–23; 8:2b–3a, 6–12, 13b, 20–22; 9:18–27; 10:8–19, 21, 24–30; 11:1–9, 28–30; 12:1–4a, 6–20; 13:1, 5, 7–11a, 12b–18; 15 mixed with E; 16:1b–2, 4–14; 18; 19:1–28, 30–38; 21:1a, 2a, 33; 22:15–18, 20–24; 24; 25:1–6, 11b, 18, 21–26a, 27–34; 26:1–33; 27:1–45; 28:10, 13–16, 19; 29:2–14, 31–35; 30:3b–5, 7, 9–16, 24–43; 31:1, 3, 46, 48–50; 32:3–13a, 22, 24–32; 33:1–17; 34:2b–3, 5, 7, 11–12, 19, 25–26, 30–31; 35:14, 21–22a; 36:15–19, 31–39; 37:3–4, 12–13, 14b, 18b, 21, 23a, 25–27, 28b, 31a, 32b–33, 35; 38; 39; 40:3b, 5b, 15b; 42:2, 4b–7, 27–28, 38; 43:1–13, 15–23a, 24–34; 44; 46:28–34; 47:1–6, 13–27a, 29–31; 49:1b–28a; 50:1–11.

Exodus: 1:6, 8–12; 2:16–23a; 3:2–4a, 5, 7–8, 16–20; 4:1–16, 19–20a, 22–31; 5; 6:1; 7:14–18, 23, 25–29; 8:4–11a, 16–28; 9:17, 13–21, 23b–34; 10:1–7, 13b–19, 28–29; 11:4–8; 12:21–27, 29–30; 13:3–16, 21–22; 14:5–7, 10–14, 19–20, 21b, 24–25, 27b, 30–31; 15:22–27; 16:4–5, 15, 19–21, 29–30; 17:1b, 2, 7; 19:20–25; 20:22–26; 24:1–2, 9–11; 32:9–14; 34:1–28.

Numbers: (with E) see below.

Deuteronomy: 34:1b–4.

Let us take up our story once again. In 931 B.C. Solomon died. Immediately the north and the south separated and formed two kingdoms: Israel in the north, where Samaria was the capital; Judah in the south, with Jerusalem as its capital.

In the north the oral traditions were set down in writing in their turn: this is the Elohist document (abbreviated E). It often deals with the same events and personages as the Yahwist document but in its own way, which we shall examine in chapter 4. Here is a table of all the Elohist passages from Genesis and Exodus. You might want to underline them in blue in your Bible.

The Elohist Document

Genesis: 15 mingled with J; 20; 21:6–32, 34; 22:1–14, 19; 28:11–12, 17–18, 20–22; 29:1, 15–23, 25–28, 30; 30:1–3a, 6, 8, 17–23; 31:2, 4–18a, 19–45, 51–55; 32:1–2, 13b–21, 23; 33:18b–20; 35:1–8, 16–20; 37:2b, 5–11, 14a, 15–18a, 19–20, 22, 23b–24, 28a, 28c–30, 31b–32a, 34, 36; 40:1–3a, 4–5a, 6–15a, 16–23; 41; 42:1,

3–4a, 8–26, 29–37; 43:14, 23b; 46:1–5a, 28–34; 47:12; 48:1–2, 8–22; 50:15–26.

Exodus: 1:15–22; 2:1–15; 3:1, 4b, 6, 9–15, 21–22; 4:17–18, 20b–21; 7:20b–21a, 24; 9:22–23a, 35; 10:8–13a, 20–27; 11:1–3; 12:31–36, 37b–39; 13:17–19; 15:1–21; 17:3–6, 8–16; 18; 19:2b–19; 20:1–21; 21; 22; 23; 24:3–8, 12–15a, 18b; 32:1–8, 15–35; 33.

Numbers: (with J) 10:29–36; 11; 12; 13:17–33 (plus P); 14 (plus P); 16:1–34 (plus P); 20:1–9, 12–35; 22; 23; 24; 25:1–5; 32:1–17, 20–27, 34–42.

Deuteronomy: 10:10, 6–7; 27:5–7a; 31:14–15, 23; 33:5–6.

However, in this northern kingdom a *prophetic movement* appeared with an *ideological* protest against religious syncretism, a *political* protest against the king and the class in power, and an *economic* protest against exploitation by the ruling class. Texts that have been handed down to us are those of the prophets Elijah and Elisha (1 Kings 17 to 2 Kings 13) and the violent discourses of Amos and Hosea. This current was expressed also in Deuteronomy 12 to 26, which is called the Deuteronomic code (abbreviated D). One finds, above all, a fairly democratic spirit that is distrustful toward the royalty and opposed to centralization; it has a very keen sense of social justice.

But in 722 B.C., the Assyrians took Samaria and destroyed the northern kingdom. A handful of people sought refuge in Jerusalem, bringing their writings, which they placed in security in the Temple.

During this time in the southern kingdom the ideological activity continued. The Proverbs and Psalms attest to the role of the scribes and cantors. Isaiah 1 to 12 shows the existence of court prophets who exalted the royal messianism. In 622 B.C., upon the fortuitous discovery of the texts carried a century earlier by the refugees from the north, the Deuteronomic reform of King Josiah took place. It is in this line that is to be situated the editing of the books of Joshua, Judges, 1 and 2 Samuel, and 1 and 2 Kings. In this spirit also, but against the background of the Babylonian invasion, are to be found the prophetic writings of Jeremiah.

In 587 B.C. the Babylonians took Jerusalem and deported the inhabitants of the kingdom of Judah to the banks of the Euphrates. During this exile of about fifty years the priests sought to assure the cohesion of the group, especially by editing the Priestly code (abbreviated P), a clerical and ritualistic version of the ancient traditions. Among other things, one finds in it the four covenants: Genesis 1, the creation; Genesis 9, the covenant with Noah; Genesis 17, the covenant with Abraham; Exodus 20 and 25 to 31, the covenant with Moses. See the following list of passages. You might want to underline them in green in your Bible.

The Priestly Document in the Pentateuch

Genesis: 1; 2:1–4a; 5:1–28, 30–32; 6:9–22; 7:6, 11, 13–16a, 18–21, 24; 8:1–2a, 3b–5, 13a, 14–19; 9:1–17, 28–29; 10:1–7, 22–23; 11:10–27, 31–32; 12:4b–5; 13:6, 11b–12a; 16:1a,3, 15–16; 17; 19:29; 21:1b, 2b–5; 23; 25:7–11a, 12–17, 19–20, 26b; 26:34–35; 27:46; 28:1–9; 29:24, 29; 31:18b; 33:18a; 34:1–2a, 4, 6, 8–10, 13–18, 20–24, 27–29; 35:9–13, 15, 22b–29; 36:1–14, 20–30, 40–43; 37:1–2a; 46:5b–27; 47:7–11, 27b–28; 48:3–7; 49:1a, 28b–33; 50:12–13.

Exodus: 1:1–5, 7, 13–14; 2:23b–25; 6:2–30; 7:1–13, 19–20a, 21b–22; 8:1–3, 11b–15; 9:8–12; 11:9–10; 12:1–20, 28, 37a, 40–51; 13:1–2, 20; 14:1–4, 8–9, 15–18, 21a, 21c–23, 26–27a, 28–29; 16:1–3, 6–14, 16–18, 22–28, 31–36; 17:1a; 19:1–2a; 24:15b–18a; 25; 26; 27; 28; 29; 30; 31:1–18a; 34:29–35; 35; 36; 37; 38; 39; 40.

All of *Leviticus*.

Numbers: 1; 2; 3; 4; 5; 6; 7; 8; 9; 10:1–28; 13:1–17a, 21, 25–26a, 32a; 14:1–2, 5–7, 10:26–30, 34–38; 15; 16:1a, 2b–11, 16–24, 27a, 32b, 35–50; 17; 18; 19; 20:1a, 3b–4, 6–13, 22–29; 21:4a, 10–11; 22:1; 25:6–18; 26; 27; 28; 29; 30; 31; 32:18–19, 28–33; 33; 34; 35; 36.

Deuteronomy: 4: 41–43; 32:48–52; 34:1a, 7–9.

In Babylon also the consolation discourses were pronounced, which make up Isaiah 40 to 55 and Ezekiel 40 to 48.[12]

In 538 B.C. Cyrus, king of the Persians and conqueror of the Babylonians, permitted the Jews to return home and to rebuild the Temple of Jerusalem. (Some Jews remained where they were or scattered across the known world: this is the Diaspora.) The activity of the clergy intensified: the first five books of the Bible (the Pentateuch) were edited for the last time on the basis of the Yahwist, Elohist, Deuteronomic, and Priestly documents. They became the Law, or Torah, and the whole history was rewritten in 1 and 2 Chronicles.

In 323 B.C. Alexander died after completely upsetting the political map of the Middle East. His lieutenants divided up his empire. Palestine came under the control of the Ptolemies of Egypt, and then of the Seleucids of Syria. One of the latter, Antiochus Epiphanes, provoked the insurrection of the Maccabees (see the books bearing the same name in the Apocrypha), while the sect of the Essenes found refuge at Qumran in the desert near the Dead Sea. During the second century B.C. *apocalyptic* texts—for example, the book of Daniel and Isaiah 24 to 27—flourished.[13]

In 63 B.C. Pompey took Jerusalem and Palestine became a Roman province. Numerous revolts broke out against the Romans: in 4 B.C. the Zealot movement began. In A.D. 66 an insurrectional government was set up in Jerusalem by the Zealots. It was wiped out by Titus in A.D. 70. The last uprising came in 132, and in 134 Hadrian razed Jerusalem and chased all the Jews from Palestine.

However, in A.D. 51 Paul wrote two epistles from Corinth to the Thessalonians. From Ephesus in A.D. 57 he wrote the first epistle to the Corinthians. From Corinth in A.D. 58 he sent the letter to the Romans. As a prisoner in Rome from A.D. 61 to 63, he wrote to the Colossians, Ephesians, and Philemon.

About A.D. 71, the Gospel according to Mark was put together in Rome. Later (about A.D. 95?) the book of Revelation by John, the Gospels of Matthew and Luke, and the Acts of the Apostles were written. Around A.D. 100 the Gospel according to John was prepared.

HOW THE SCRIPTURES BECAME THE BIBLE

This brief historical reminder suffices perhaps to show the process by which the production of writings that constitute the Bible took place.

What already appears clearly is that these texts were produced by different and opposing social groups, and that their various overhaulings up to the definitive edition also may be understood as the work of particular social groups. It remains for us, therefore, to search for the dialectics of these different groups in order to understand the role and function of their textual production.

In addition, we pose the hypothesis that historical materialism was operative (or functioned as the explicating system) even for precapitalist societies. Publications of the Center of Marxist Studies and Research[14] and the book *For History*[15] by Guy Dhoquois furnish us the means of analyzing the history of Israel at the economic, political, and ideological levels and of linking them in order to discern the class struggles. Thus the Scriptures, understood as the ideological production of definite social groups, can enlighten us about their own conditions of production, circulation, and consumption.

To situate each text historically, we often shall use the publications of modern exegetical scholars.[16] But we shall try to go further and to see how and to what measure the conditions of production determined the function of these writings. Thus perhaps we will escape making an idealist reading, for which the Bible is a kind of sacred word more or less straight from heaven.

This conception is itself rooted in history: it is the priestly caste in power in Jerusalem at the return from Exile (after 538 B.C.) which transformed the ancient traditions into "the Law of God." The priestly caste even persuaded the Persian ruler that the Jewish Law should be considered the law of the king, which was to be imposed in an authoritarian way upon all the inhabitants of Palestine (Esdras 7:26). And when this law was translated into Greek at Alexandria (about 250 B.C.), the author of the Letter of Aristeas[17] declared: "This legislation is holy and is the work of God."

A century later one of the Maccabee brothers, Jonathan, writing to the Spartans, spoke to them of the holy books (I Macc. 12:9)—in Greek *biblia*—which were the consolation of the resistance. It is this Greek term, in the neuter plural, which was later translated into Latin as *biblia* (feminine singular) and became *the Bible*. One sees the shrinking process that took place: during many centuries all sorts of texts were produced and circulated among the people—legends, historical records, customs, laws, songs, poems, oracles, stories. Little by little the class in power established an official canon—or approved collection—of which the prologue of Ecclesiasticus (written in 132 B.C.) gave the divisions that were to become classic: "the Law, the prophets, and the other writers."

The same mechanism was to function for the texts of the New Testament (cf. the Muratorium canon of about A.D. 180).[18] In addition the ecclesiastical authorities will tend more and more to reserve to themselves the exclusive privilege of interpretation of the "right" reading. Thus Tertullian around A.D. 200 addressed himself in these terms to the "heretic" Marcion: "By what right do you cut trees in my forest? It is I who am the heir of the apostles; I possess the Scripture, and I am the only one to possess it."[19]

The climax of the success of the dominant ideology was expressed in A.D. 434 by Vincent de Lerins, summing up the meaning of the "true" interpretation of the Bible as follows: "The rule must be what has been believed everywhere, always, and by everybody."[20] As if the texts did not witness precisely to different beliefs and practices, products of the social groups struggling against one another! We know that the thrust of every dominant ideology is to present itself and to impose itself as the One, universal, and eternal.

One of the aims of our book is to dismantle this ideology, this idealist reading of the Bible. We do it from the real situation (in a materialist sense) of present-day struggles, specifically against the apparatus of ecclesiastical politics.[21]

Chapter 2

The Scriptures Begin with Solomon

The Bible you have in your hands presents the scriptures in a certain order: the Old Testament begins with Genesis and ends with Malachi; the New Testament puts in first place the Gospel according to Matthew and in last place Revelation or the Apocalypse. But this seemingly chronological order is entirely arbitrary; in fact, it has changed throughout the centuries, except for the first five books (the Pentateuch).

We have stated that our method consists in regarding the biblical texts as ideological products of well-defined social groups and, consequently in analyzing their conditions of production.

The first consequence is that we must begin our work with the texts that were produced the earliest, with, those that to be precise, were *written* the earliest. Of course, we recognize that most of them transcribe traditions, myths, and oral accounts that were often very old. But we are committed to study the conditions of the *written* production of the Bible, because we believe that it is this *process of writing* that will enlighten us about its function.

Specialists in the study of the Bible (who are often great scholars, even if they do not always take into account the ideology in which they are functioning) are in agreement in saying that one of the very first *written* texts of the Bible is the "narration of the succession of David" (2 Sam. 9–20; and 1 Kings 1–2).[1] We shall consider therefore that the scriptures of Israel begin with this text, and we shall study it more closely.[2]

13

A VERY OFFICIAL ROYAL CHRONICLE

In any text the first and last sentences are always very important: they indicate generally not only the beginning and the end but also the essential characteristics of the text. Thus fairy tales begin with the ritual phrases "once upon a time" and conclude often with the formula "and they lived happily ever after." Similarly in music a symphony begins with a chord that gives the tone of the piece and ends not surprisingly in the same tone. That allows readers and hearers to situate themselves, to know what is happening and what is the product offered to them. In the same way, at the movies a film begins usually (and the exceptions owe their surprise effect to the rule) with the title and credits, and concludes with the words "The End."

The account of the succession of David does not have such a title in the Bible. It has no title at all. It is inserted in the middle of other texts, and it is located especially by its first and last sentences. Here is the first sentence: "David asked: Is any member of Saul's family left?" (2 Sam. 1:1). And this is the last sentence: "Thus Solomon's royal power was securely established" (1 Kings 2:46).

In brief, the role of our text is to make the connection between these two sentences, to go from one to the other without a hitch, more exactly to move the reader from one to the other as naturally as possible, as if there were no problem. But there is one, to be sure; otherwise the text would never have existed. It responds like every ideological product to a specific need: in this case *to recount in a certain manner* a historical period, to render this version credible, to impose it. In its own way it functions like the *Commentaries* of Julius Caesar concerning the war in Gaul or the *War Memoirs* of General de Gaulle: the attempt is made to give credit to one's own version of the facts.

What facts are involved? Our two sentences show us: *the manner in which David, then Solomon, succeeded Saul on the royal throne.* Before going further, we suggest that you read the whole passage. It is fairly short and as fascinating as an adventure story: David's war against the Ammonites, his adultery with Bathsheba, the story of Absalom's conspiracy, the old age and death of

David, Solomon's ascension to the throne—all these episodes will keep you in suspense (2 Sam. 9–10 and 1 Kings 1–2).

One becomes absorbed by the story, believes it! Let us try now to be less naive: why does the text begin by having David ask about the possible survivors of Saul's family? Remember what we said in chapter 1: Saul had been elected king by the tribes of the north. At his death David succeeded in having himself named king, first by the tribes of the south (Judah) and then by those of the north (Israel). But that must not have happened easily, and David must have feared above everything else that some sons of Saul might challenge his power in the north. Fortunately for him, the sons of Saul were killed one after another (as other texts show: 2 Sam. 4:7 for Ishbosheth, 2 Sam. 21:9 for seven other sons). When he raised the question, David had before him only Mephibosheth, grandson of Saul, who was crippled and therefore could not hope to reign. David could sleep peacefully.

But to tell the truth, it is not the succession of Saul that the text wished to relate to us but that of David, that is to say, the access of Solomon to the throne. The last sentence of the account is unmistakable in that respect. Consequently this introduction centered on David teaches primarily one thing, which is that the problem for Solomon had been the same as that for David—how to gain the throne by cutting off the other pretenders. To become aware of this more precisely, we only need to trace the genealogical chart of David's family, taking the names given in our text:

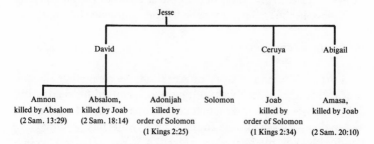

Thus the three older brothers of Solomon and his two cousins were slain very conveniently. But the trap in this text is precisely that it tells this in such a manner as to make these deaths seem perfectly natural, without any relation to David's succession. It is our reading that makes the text confess that its purpose is to hide something. And we can understand why the exegetes date this text from the period of Solomon:[3] it was produced certainly by order of the king, by one (or several) court scribes with a view to furnishing the official history of the Davidic dynasty.

THE BIRTH OF A STATE

The account of the succession of David was therefore a product of Solomon's monarchy. But the opposite is also true: the power of Solomon was in a way produced by the account. On the ideological level (the representation or idea that people make of the world in which they live), this account furnished the framework in which contemporaries and all readers later on were obliged to read the history of this reign. To make a materialist reading (which avoids this ideology), we must unravel this text for every text is a textile, a tissue of interwoven threads. We must see what it reveals about its conditions of production. As Jean-Pierre Faye states, "Since history is made only in the telling, a critique of history can only be made in recounting how history, in being told, is produced.[4]

We have posed the hypothesis that every society (or "social formation") is a complex system of exchanges on three levels: the economic, political, and ideological.

Produced by (and for) the new Solomonic State, our text must furnish us, therefore, signs at these three levels of the change that took place in the social formation by the emergence of a State.

Economic Exchanges

In the very romantic story of Absalom, we remember the episode of his hair, which was so long that it caused his death. But did you observe this little sentence: "When he cut his hair (as he had to do every year for he found it heavy), his hair weighed two hundred shekels by the royal standard" (2 Sam. 14:26)? This sentence indicates a turning point in the development of economic exchanges. To understand its meaning, we turn to Marx. At the beginning of *Das Kapital,*[5] he analyzed in four steps the historical development of economic exchanges:

1. One merchandise is set in a value relation with another; it is a trade: I exchange an ox for a sheep.

2. One merchandise is set in a value relation with all others; I perceive that my ox can be exchanged for anything: an ax, a donkey, some wheat, and so on.

3. All merchandise expresses its value in a single merchandise taken as a *general equivalent*, which normalizes henceforth all exchanges; my neighbors and I agree that my ox is worth so much (shekels, for example) and can be exchanged for something of equal worth or which can be multiplied (an ox of ten shekels is worth five objects of two shekels).

4. A single form, gold, functions as the universal general equivalent and sets the value of all the merchandise; it is the modern money-form.

Our text clearly indicates the third stage: the shekels by the royal standard were the *general equivalent* that normalized the weights and measures, that is to say, the economic exchanges. But what interests us particularly is that this unity of standards is indicated as fixed by the king: that means that the birth of the Davidic monarchy was marked here on the economic level by the fact that all the exchanges were henceforth to be controlled by the royal power.

Thus everything was interrelated: as economics and politics (and, we shall see, ideology) were only mutually dependent aspects or instances of a social reality.[6]

Political Exchanges

We shall verify all the above concepts on the political level. Our text gives us three pieces of information, among others:

—*Geographic centralization.* If we follow on a map of Palestine all the journeyings of the personages of the story, we see that they all passed through Jerusalem, a city which did not belong either to the group of tribes in the north or to those of the south, and which David had made his capital. We know from modern linguistics that language is a system of oppositional relations:[7] for example, when I say, "I am here," this means also "I am not elsewhere." Therefore, if the text signaled Jerusalem as the crossroads of all important routes, it was not by chance. On the other hand, the travels of people in a country spring from the political factor that determines specifically the places of members in the society. Thus the centralization of geographic exchanges by the royal capital symbolized perfectly the fact that the political exchanges passed from that time on through the king.

—*Administrative centralization.* 2 Samuel 20:23–26 furnishes the list of the great officers of David: the commander-in-chief of the army, the head of the royal guard, the director of recruitment, the herald, the scribe, and the priests. Army, police, administration, clergy—this was a summing up of the new class in power. Guy Dhoquois' analyses concerning the precapitalist societies enable us to understand better what is going on here.[8] The instant peasant clans became organized militarily against the Philistines, this new class (for example, the commander-in-chief of the army) became necessary. But it took advantage in extending the system of taxation and forced labor (thus the head of the forced labor and of the local armed units) and therefore for controlling exchanges at the three levels, that is to merge with the state. This is why Dhoquois speaks of the class-state. Since there did not exist in Palestine the possibility of major public works (especially irrigation), as in Egypt and in Mesopotamia, the social formation was not exactly *Asian* (a class-state rendered necessary by the centralization of the productive labor forces) but *sub-Asian* (the class-state imposing itself only at the level of the relationships of production, i.e., controlling the exchanges). It was, therefore, in the opposition of the village tribes to the class-state that the class struggle manifested itself.[9] Since this was added to the resistance of the tribes of the north against those of the south (David was from the south), the struggle was expressed notably by the revolt of the men of Israel (therefore from the north) following Sheba (2 Sam. 20:1–2) and, finally, by the north-south schism which came to pass at Solomon's death precisely due to a military draft (1 Kings 12:16).

—*Juridical centralization.* "Every man that had a case to bring before the king for judgment . . ." (2 Sam. 15:2). Thus is indicated the creation of royal tribunals, charged with setting the equivalence between offenses and indemnities, and unifying judgment. It is stage three of the evolution of law, after the primitive vendetta (stage one) and the system of penalties like the Code of Hammurabi (stage two) and before the establishment of universal judicial system (stage four). Our text indicates clearly that the state apparatus has been set up in a similar way at every level. On the political level, it was the *king* who held the role of *general equivalent*.

Ideological Exchanges

The ideological products (myths, narratives, and speeches) by which people give themselves a way to read, that is, to understand, their own social practice are taken for the most part from the ideology of the dominant class.

—*Religion*. Our account gives little room to religion; this is normal, because in presenting itself as the historical chronicle, it cannot have someone from outside intervene in the narrative, *deus ex machina* who would seem to be pulling the strings backstage. To be credible, a historical account must follow the rule of the unexpected, that is to say, the risks; the historical account is of interest only if one does not know the outcome. But by definition God is he who knows (the beginning and) the end of history. This is why the episode of Bathsheba is particularly significant (2 Sam. 12).

In fact, in all of our text this is the passage where the religious marks are most visible. "What David had done displeased Yahweh" (2 Sam. 11:27); sent Nathan the prophet to David" (12:1); Nathan spoke abundantly in the name of Yahweh (12:5, 7, 9, 11, 13, 14); "Yahweh struck the child" (12:15); "Yahweh loved him" (Solomon, the second child of Bathsheba) (12:24). The commentators of the Bible are always ecstatic over the personage of David, a great lover and awful sinner who was magnificent in repentance. Let us note rather the first and last sentences: "What David had done displeased Yahweh" and "Yahweh loved Solomon." The passage between the sentences had the purpose of linking them. For the scribe of Solomon it was a matter of officially rendering plausible the fact that the king was loved by God (and not just any God, but by "Yahweh, God of Israel," the god of the northern tribes!). And this was so even though Solomon was not a legitimate descendant of David but a son by adultery.

Thus our text shows itself to be an ideological production, having for its purpose the religious legitimizing of the Solomonic power by leaning for support on the sacred traditions of the tribes, especially those of the north from whom the Ark of the Covenant had been transported by David to his capital at Jerusalem.[10]

—*Literature.* The very existence of our text is proof of a literary activity at Solomon's court. In the list of great officers of the king (2 Sam. 20:25), a secretary is mentioned, who was the head of service for the scribes. (Moreover, he has an Egyptian name, a sign of the probable influence of the political alliances of Solomon, who had married a daughter of the Pharaoh.) The writing down in an official version of the ancient traditions of the tribes performed on the ideological level the same work of centralization, of legitimizing, of consolidating power by a general equivalent. Henceforth, the relation of the tribes to their past was to be governed by the written text, which has the power of law to such a point that the day will come, after the Exile, when it was to be called the Law.

We have verified our hypothesis: the setting down in writing of the Bible began under the reign of Solomon and at his initiative. It is therefore with regard to this perspective that it must be read.

Chapter 3

The Royal Court of Solomon and the J Document

Biblical scholars call the product of the work of the scribes of Solomon the Yahwist document (abbreviated J). The reason is that the divinity is always named Yahweh there, as opposed to the Elohist document (E) where the word *elohim* (gods) is used up to the time when Moses learned the name of Yahweh.

Rather than follow all the J passages from Genesis and Exodus, we shall try to show their structure and *raison d'être*.

ELEMENTS

What elements did the scribes of Solomon have? There were two kinds, essentially: from the south and from the north.

South

In fact, David and Solomon were part of the house of Judah, the group of clans inhabiting the mountain of Judah, between Hebron and Bethlehem. They were the descendants of Semitic tribes chased out of Egypt which, after a time at the oasis of Kadesh, had entered Canaan from the south. They conserved the memory of the great ancestors who were more or less legendary: Abraham whose memory was venerated at Hebron (they still showed the oak woods of Mamre where he had pitched his tent); Isaac whose tradition was rooted in Beersheba.[1]

21

North

The main political problem of David and Solomon, as we have seen, was the autonomist tendency of the tribes in the north. They were descendants of groups which had left Egypt with Moses and which, instead of fleeing northward and entering Canaan from the south, had headed east through the Sinai Desert and had finally penetrated into Canaan by fording the Jordan. There, under the leadership of Joshua, these tribes had formed a kind of confederation, the Shechem Covenant. The spirit of nomad independence was still strong, and they had only accepted the royalty of Saul under military pressure from the Philistines. The creation of the Davidic-Solomonic state, which imposed taxes and forced labor, encountered resistance among these people who bore the name of a glorious ancestor, Israel.

CONSTRUCTION

With all these elements, the royal scribes performed a rather complex work of interweaving in order to make a single history of various traditions.

The Same Ancestors

First of all, they tied together the two ancestors, Abraham and Israel, making Isaac the father of one and the son of the other. They then put the same personage under the double name of Israel and Jacob; and the twelve sons became the eponymous ancestors of the twelve tribes that formed the double kingdom of Israel and Judah.[2]

The Same Land

Here the work of the scribes can be traced by looking at the map. Observe the travels of the two patriarchs. Before arriving at Hebron, which is his place, Abraham passed through Shechem and Bethel, places that belong to the traditions concerning Jacob-Israel, and through Beersheba, the place of Isaac. As for Jacob-Israel, the text puts him in a family relationship with the Arameans (among whom he took his wives) and the Edomites (through the personage of his brother Esau). In fact, these two peoples had been conquered and subjected by David (2 Sam. 8, 6, 14).

To sum up, everything happens as if our scribes used a geographic thread to sew together the different pieces, Abraham and Jacob serving as needle or shuttle.

The Same Promises

The J Document has many promises addressed to the patriarchs: to Abraham (Genesis 12:1–3;15: 3–5;18 to 21); to Rebecca (Genesis 25:23); to Isaac (Genesis 26:24); to Jacob (Genesis 27:28–29); to Jacob's sons (Genesis 49); (cf. The Song of Deborah: Judges 5, and the Oracle of Balaam: Numbers 24). What is it that is promised? A *land*, whose limits were precisely those of the kingdom of Solomon; an *heir*, who was never the first-born son (Isaac over Ishmael; Jacob over Esau; Judah over Joseph). In short, everything occurs as if Solomon had caused the history of the patriarchs to be written with a view to his own history and to the double necessity of legitimizing his ascension to the throne and of justifying his domination over the tribes of the north and the neighboring peoples.

The Same Liberation from Egypt

It is rather difficult to trace the J document in Exodus, first because after the burning bush episode E and J both speak of Yahweh, but especially because the traditions of the departure from Egypt with Moses belonged to the northern tribes, and the scribes of Solomon must have had difficulty reworking them in their style. In fact, most biblical scholars[3] emphasize that, during the whole time of the royalty, Mount Sinai was more or less eclipsed by Mount Zion on, which Jerusalem is built, with its temple to which David had the Ark of the northern tribes carried. We shall see that a part of the prophetic movement originating in the north was to struggle to lift up again the traditions of the desert against royal centralization.

However, the J document also has its Exodus or liberation

from Egypt. This would seem strange when we remember that the southern tribes left Egypt at a different time and entered Canaan by a different route from the tribes of the north guided by Moses. The southern tribes were not present at the Assembly of Shechem (Josh. 24), which sealed the confederation of the northern tribes and their faith in "Yahweh who has saved us from Egypt." Father de Vaux explains that the two groups that left Egypt must have met for a time at the Kadesh oasis.[4] Can we be sure of this? We could also suppose that the royal scribes wanted to take over the northern traditions. A few clues show their work, in fact. Thus the personage of Moses is presented by J as the liberator of Israel, the royal title (cf. 2 Kings 13:5); he decrees laws (the word means "royal edict" Exod. 15:25); and he is surrounded by notables (Exod. 24:11) similar to the royal officers of David and Solomon.

The Same Politics

A particular episode of the J document in the book of the Exodus deserves our attention for a moment. Exodus 47:13-26 shows, in effect, the agrarian politics undertaken by Joseph, one of the sons of Jacob-Israel and an eponymous ancestor of the northern tribes, who became prime minister of the Pharaoh. He took advantage of a prolonged famine to buy from the Egyptians their cattle, then their lands, and then themselves, whom he reduced to serfdom. Now we shall see, in studying the E document, this was precisely the politics which the people of the north accused the royal state of having implemented at their expense (cf. 1 Sam. 8). It is, therefore, interesting to see the scribes of Solomon put on the shoulders of Joseph, the ancestor of the tribes of the north exploited by Solomon, the very principle of these politics.

The Same God

If the relationship Abraham-Isaac-Jacob was a product of the J authors, even more so was the God of Abraham, of Isaac, and of Jacob—the God who spoke to Moses (Exod. 3:16). It is perfectly obvious that the patriarchs each had separate and distinct gods to whom the text still witnessed in the title of the holy places where their memory was honored: El Shaddai at Hebron, El Olam at Beersheba, and El Berith at Shechem. In making a single god out of all the local divinities and in giving him the name Yahweh, which is in a way the secret of the Elohist document, the J document assimilated the traditions of the northern tribes and tried to reinforce the political power of Solomon by basing it on a unified religious ideology that, thus idealized, that would give him a better grip on power.

Myths Made Real

The Semitic tribes were never much interested in mythical legends of the origin of the world. The northern traditions testify that for them history began with the liberation from Egypt. But the royal scribes, like all their Babylonian and Egyptian colleagues whose influence we have already noted, sought to place the historical chronicle which they had elaborated in the majestic framework of the overall history of the world. Thus they had to apply themselves to filling the vacuum between the most ancient personage of their chronicle—Abraham—and the beginning of the universe. The epic myths of Gilgamesh and of Atra-Hasis must have served as models.[5] But they still did not forget Solomon and their concerns. The role of Eve touched on the importance of women in the problems of succession (Sarah, Rebecca, Rachel, Leah, and Bathsheba). The rivalry of Cain and Abel recalled that of younger brothers with the firstborn up through Solomon. The three sons of Noah enabled them to place the Semites, who were descendants of Shem, above the Canaanites, the descendants of Ham, and alongside the Philistines, the descendants of Japheth— a situation that is obviously that of the beginning of the Davidic dynasty.

Thus the history of Israel from the creation to Solomon seems to focus the divine attention on the personage announced with such phrases as "he who will crush the serpents' head" (Gen. 3:15), "he whose scepter will never pass away and whom the nations will obey" (Gen. 49:10), "the hero who will rule over numerous peoples, a greater king than Agag" (Num. 24:7), "a star coming forth from Jacob" (Num. 24:17), that is to say, King Solomon. In fact, that is the conclusion of the exegete H. Cazelles:

According to what remains [of the J document], it would
seem that its purpose was to begin with the oral and written
traditions, patriarchal or Mosaic, in establishing the legitimacy of the successor of the great unifier of the
land of Israel conquered by the tribes.[6]

Which does not prevent him from adding:

The problems of his time are not ours; his contemporaries
easily accepted the supernatural, which ours reject; . . .
thus it seems that the best way to approach him is to have in
mind a notion of mystery similar to the Christian notion.[7]

It is certain that the contemporaries of Solomon (and of Abraham, if he existed) were steeped in the sacred and did not distinguish between religion and politics. But our analysis of the
Yahwist document has led us to see there an ideological enterprise
of the state whose political function interests us here more than
the religious meaning. To read it in the first degree as a beautiful
story of a series of divine promises fulfilled by the coming to
power of Solomon would be to fall into his trap. To escape, we
must confront J with E, which is a witness of the traditions of the
northern tribes dominated awhile by David and Solomon, and
which recovered their independence at the latter's death.

Chapter 4

The Prophetic Milieu in the North, the E and D Documents, and the System of Gift

THE TEN TRIBES OF THE NORTH

We have seen that the tribes that left Egypt under Moses entered Canaan with Joshua and settled in the north (more precisely in the center of the country), particularly in the mountain of Ephraim. They constituted a kind of confederation—"the house of Joseph" or "of Israel"—whose main sanctuary was at Shechem. The united kingdom of David and Solomon (1000–931 B.C.) joined by force Israel (the north) to Judah (the south), but Israel kept its specificity and accepted this unification with difficulty, as shown by Sheba's revolt under David (2 Sam. 20:1–2) and Jeroboam's under Solomon (1 Kings 11:26–40). This was even more the case because the house of Joseph was subjected to the labor draft, which was not the case with Judah (1 Kings 5:14; 11:28). Judah benefited also from a special administration, which was different from the twelve prefectures set up to oversee the country and to assure the collection of taxes and the raising of soldiers (1 Kings 4:7–19).

The most classical historians confirm this situation:

The glory of the reign of Solomon, which is reflected in the official literature of royal Jerusalem, rested on a mer-

27

cantile prosperity resulting from control of the commercial routes. The wealth thus acquired could not benefit the people as a whole. On the contrary, it must have accentuated the differences between classes of Israelite society by favoring the large landholders able to invest their money in commercial ventures. The administrative system David began to set up resulted in the formation of an elite of dignitaries and royal functionaries numbering among the privileged. That is the principle of the long social crises that mark the history of the ninth and eighth centuries. But the first crisis was above all political. For the enlistment of men and money necessary for the construction of the Temple, the upkeep of the court and the royal army, Solomon did not hesitate to exploit the territories of the northern tribes, richer and more populous than Judah which, as the royal tribe, must have enjoyed certain privileges. The purpose of the prefectures (1 Kings 4:7–19) was to impose the authority of the king on those regions, without paying attention to the traditional tribal borders, in order to make tax collection and recruitment easier. In these conditions, it is not surprising that the Solomonic power should appear as despotism and that the unity between Israel and Judah in the person of David should break up at the death of his son. Toward 922 B.C. [we would say rather in 931] an Ephraimite named Jeroboam, who had revolted already against Solomon, pushed the northern tribes to secede and founded a kingdom of Israel, independent of the kingdom of Judah, where Reboboam, son of Solomon, reigned.[1]

Thus Israel returns "to its tents" (1 Kings 12:16). Let us examine its situation more closely, at the three levels of the economy, politics, and ideology.

Economy

After a period of weakness (from which David and Solomon profited), Egypt and Assyria recovered a new expansiveness; wars followed upon wars. Also the kingdom of Israel (like Judah) was constrained to pay heavy tribute to foreign sovereigns. The economic situation, therefore, was difficult.[2] It contributed to the accentuation of class differences; the rich exploited ever more severely the poor peasants, who were subjected to exorbitant interest rates (50 to 100 percent) which often led them to abandon their lands and to become slaves. In addition, flooded by foreign products, the country offered little industrial or commercial employment. Salaried workers worked by the day and without any guarantee from one day to the next: seasonable unemployment was considerable. In the face of that, the luxury of the rich, of the dignitaries, of the merchants and landholders, insolently expanded (see Amos 3:15; 5:7-13; 6:4-6). Thus the secession of the northern tribes had resulted in reconstituting a sub-Asian society more or less similar to the united kingdom of Solomon. There were some differences, however.

Politics

In effect, Israel did not reproduce purely and simply the monarchical system of Solomon. Referring back to Saul, the king of the north who was designated by the prophet Samuel and acclaimed by the people (1 Sam. 10), the Israelites chose Jeroboam, who was designated by the prophet Ahijah (1 Kings 11:29-39): "They called him to the assembly and made him king over Israel" (1 Kings 12:20). The dynastic principle was abandoned, therefore, for designation by a prophet and by the people. This was to introduce into the political power a permanent element of discontinuity and trouble. Conspiracies, rebellions, and assassinations multiplied: there were no less than nineteen kings of Israel in two centuries (931-722 B.C.).

Ideology

The tribes of the north had affirmed at Shechem that their God was "Yahweh who saved us from Egypt" (Josh. 24). The old traditions of the desert were still strong there: the spirit of the clan was ferociously democratic (this was an anachronism, but a rather symbolic one). It was hostile to all centralization, especially of the holy places, and to all monopolizing of power.

This state of mind was expressed for a long time in the north by the intermediary of personages called prophets; the whole history of Israel was stamped by their adventures.

Already in the time of Moses seventy elders (heads of clans) were invested with the prophetic spirit and Moses exclaimed: "Ah, if only the whole people of the Lord could be prophets!" (Num. 11:4–30).

At the time of the judges (because "in those days there was no king in Israel and each one did what was right in his own eyes" [Judg. 21:25]), the prophetess Deborah sang about the volunteers of the people (i.e., the mass uprising of the peasants) and the chiefs of the northern tribes (Judg. 5).

A little later, at the time of Abimelech's attempt to be king, Jotham spoke his fable (Judg. 9:7 15), which has been called the most violent antimonarchic pamphlet in the world's literature.

Under the pressure of the Philistines, the Israelites gave themselves a king, Saul. He mixed in with a band of prophets and prophesied with them (1 Sam. 10:9–12). This did not indicate that Saul belonged to such prophetic groups, but that he was at least familiar with them.

But the prophet Samuel was hostile to the kingship, and before anointing Saul carefully warned the tribes against the demands that the king would make them suffer (1 Sam. 8).

At the end of the reign of Solomon, Ahijah, the prophet of Shiloh in the north, told Jeroboam, the head of the forced levy of the house of Joseph, that he was chosen by Yahweh to govern the ten tribes "torn out of the hand of Solomon" (1 Kings 11:29–39).

Likewise, the prophet Jehu, son of Hanani, announced that King Baasha would be "swept away" (1 Kings 16:1–7). And the prophet Micaiah, son of Imlah, predicted to King Ahab his defeat and death (1 Kings 22:1–37).

It was precisely under the reign of Ahab (874–853 B.C.) that perhaps the greatest prophet of all, Elijah the Tishbite of Gilead, appeared. Elijah very violently opposed the king and his wife, Jezebel, daughter of the king of Phoenicia. (She was also the mother of the Athalie of Racine's great play.) The episode of Naboth's vineyard (1 Kings 21) was a characteristic example of arbitrary royalty challenged by the prophets.

Presented as a disciple and successor of Elijah, Elisha lived in a community of a very picturesque brotherhood of prophets, which was somewhat "hippy." He stirred up a revolt against the successor of Ahab and designated Jehu to take the power and reestablish the worship of Yahweh (2 Kings 9–10).

It was probably at this time (about 850) that the traditions of the northern tribes began to be written down.[3] They made up the Elohist (E) document and later were integrated into the Pentateuch by the postexilic priests.

THE E DOCUMENT

The northern prophetic milieus that produced this document already knew the J document, at least as much of it as then existed. They therefore chose to follow the main thread, modifying it or completing it as they went along. Thus in reading E, we can discover the characteristics of the northern ideology.

First of all, E begins its account directly with Abraham (Gen. 15), without borrowing as J does from the Egyptian and Mesopotamian scribes a cosmological introduction about the creation of the world.

It clearly appears that E is the story of the house of Joseph. This personage has a considerable role in this story (Gen. 37–50). Moses carried along the remains of Joseph when he fled Egypt (Exod. 13:17). And Joseph's "sons" (the tribes of Ephraim and Manasseh) dominated the center of the country and imposed their power and their religion on others at the assembly of Shechem (Josh. 16, 17, 24).

The people hold a larger place in E than in J. They are called "the children of Israel" (Exod. 3:9, 13, etc.); they are organized in groups judged by "capable men, God-fearing, honest and incorruptible" (Exod. 18:21); it is with them, the people, that Yahweh covenants and not directly with Moses, as J has it (Exod. 24:3–8).

Furthermore, for E Moses was above all a prophet who was superior to Aaron and Myriam, it is true (Num. 12:6–8), but one who shared the spirit of Yahweh with the elders of Israel (Num. 11:16–17). And Abraham himself was presented as a prophet (Gen. 20:7). These are the personages who served as intermediaries for the covenants between Yahweh and the people. It is striking, moreover, to find often for these covenants the ceremony that must have been practiced for a long time at Shechem for the renewal of the confederation pact among the northern tribes (Exod. 24:4, 7–8; cf. Josh. 4:1–5; 8:30–35; 24; cf. Deut. 27; cf. also Elijah in 1 Kings 18:30–31).

As for the legislative system that serves as a reference for the E document, it was the Covenant Code, sealed at Mount Horeb by Moses (Exod. 21–23: 19), consisting of civil and penal law, and rules for worship and social morality. Those customs or "words" spoke neither of a king nor of state justice nor of an organized clergy. They recognized a plurality of sanctuaries; they held to the law of revenge and anathema, which Elijah applied to the worshipers of Baal (1 Kings 18:40) as well as to Jehu (2 Kings 10:18–27). We shall see with the Deuteronomic Code what was the role and function of this legislative system.

Another peculiarity of the E document must be noted: the name of God remained secret, and it was forbidden to see him. It was through dreams that he spoke to Abraham, Abimeleck, Jacob, and Joseph. He refused to give his name to Jacob (Gen. 32:30–31) and said to Moses only: "I am; that is who I am" (Exod. 3:14), thereby preventing people from having a hold on him and from using him. (It is true that the four consonants YHWH can be interpreted differently.)

THE DEUTERONOMIC CODE AND THE SYSTEM OF GIFT

Chapters 12 to 26 of Deuteronomy must have been produced in the same milieus and about the same period as the E document.[4] But since they make up especially the Covenant Code, we shall look at them more in detail. In fact, one can consider them as the basic text regulating human relations in the perspective of the prophetic milieus of the north.

For those peasant clans which kept alive the memory of the life in the desert and which waited upon heaven for the sun and rain, *life was first of all a gift.* And social life—the possibility of living in peace among the clans—depended on reciprocal giving. Because Yahweh had given the country to his people, no one could take over the land: "that there will never be any poor among you" (Deut. 15:4).

We can examine these features in detail in the three areas of social life: food, family, worship, which are the three sectors of production, circulation, and consumption. They include supplies, bodies, and religious objects (prayers, sacrifices, and tithes).

Food

All those who had no means of subsistence—Levites, foreigners, widows, and orphans—had a right to a triennial tithe as well as to the leavings of the harvest. Pawn for loans were not to be forfeited. Interest-bearing loans were forbidden. Day laborers had to be paid each evening. Debtors fallen into slavery had to be freed at the end of seven years. And the Decalogue of Deuteronomy 5, taking up that of Exodus 21, of course forbade theft and even covetousness of one's neighbor's wife, house, field, man servant or woman servant, ox or ass. To transgress these laws was to become a debtor of another, and of God, the author of every gift.

Family

In contrast to our contemporary concern for the population explosion, the Israelites, like all ancient peoples, sought to assure the continuity of life by having a wife or wives and children who would prolong the existence of the "name." The prohibitions thus bear on adultery (taking the wife of another), murder (the major violence against life, the supreme debt), and slander or false witness (which stained the honor of the name).

Worship

Since every gift came from Yahweh, it was to him, the one God of Israel, that everything returned. The first obligation was thus to eliminate the cult objects of other gods, and to offer sacrifices, burnt offerings, and tithes to Yahweh. This feast for Yahweh, which constituted the sacrifice, the consummation of what was usually consumed, was in effect the essence of the sacred. But what seems specific in our texts is the insistence on the fact that the way to be in contact with Yahweh was not through idols and images (Deut. 4:15–20; 27:15), but through the narration of his power at work in the midst of his people. Thus, for example:

> When your son asks you in time to come, "What is the meaning of the precepts, statutes and laws which the Lord our God gave you?", you shall say to him: "We were Pharaoh's slaves in Egypt, and the Lord brought us out of Egypt with his strong hand, sending great disasters, signs and portents against the Egyptians and against Pharaoh and all his family, as we saw for ourselves. But he led us out from there to bring us into the land and give it to us, as he had promised to our forefathers. The Lord commanded us to observe all these statutes and to fear the Lord our God; it will be for our own good at all times, and he will continue to preserve our lives" [Deut. 6:20–24, cf. 8:12–18 and 26:5–9].

Thus, the *narration* of the powerful practice of Yahweh structured the faith of his people. The narration of this founding gesture remained open to history as it was taking place and to the narration of the practices of the people "today" (this is one of the key words of the Deuteronomist).

Moreover, in function of this demand the Deuteronomic Code defined the statute of the king. Chosen by Yahweh "from among the brethren," he was not to multiply his horses and his wives nor his gold; he was not to become proud above his brothers (Deut. 17:14–20). And this is also why the Deuteronomic Code was summed up in the famous commandment: "Hear, O Israel, the Lord is our God, one Lord, and you must love the Lord your God with all your heart and soul and strength" (Deut. 6:4–5). In effect, to love is to give; to give life is to deny death; to increase in wealth does not prevent having to die. To give is the only way if life, after all, is to continue.

It was on this basis that was built the willingness to live together of the northern tribes.

Chapter 5

The Priestly Caste, the P Document, and the System of Purity

It will be remembered that when Jerusalem fell into the hands of the Babylonians in 587 B.C., a part of the population was deported to the banks of the Euphrates. It is important to point out that those people were essentially the ruling classes and the priests, Levites, and scribes. The little people of the countryside, however, were left in place.[1] This is often overlooked, since those people who could not read and write have left no trace of their existence, except perhaps the Lamentations traditionally attributed to Jeremiah. At the same time, the exiles of the rivers of Babylon (see Ps. 137) wrote so well that in the Bible they were the ones who became, in fact, the people of Israel.

In the debacle of the deportation, it was the priests who constituted the moral girders, as it were. They restored the meaning of traditional practices that symbolized the attachment to Israel: the Sabbath and circumcision. But especially they created religious assemblies from which came the synagogues where the old records were read and commented upon, though in a new perspective. It was imperative, above all, to forget none of the prescriptions and prohibitions of what was called the Law or Torah.

In this setting chapters 40 to 48 of Ezekiel ("The Torah of Eze-kiel") were produced, which so forcefully imagined details of the future restoration of Israel and the reconstruction of the Temple. Likewise, in this context chapters 17 to 26 of Leviticus ("The Ho-liness Law"), were written; they accented what had then become the principal characteristic of Judaism: ritual, moral, and social purity. Finally, this was where the Priestly document (abbre-viated P) began to develop.[2]

THE P DOCUMENT AND THE LAW

P is a kind of catechism. It begins with a vast and magnificent picture of the universe: chapter 1 of Genesis, which is the first page of our Bible and doubtless the best known. In fact, it is the first of the genealogies that constitute the framework of the P document. There are also those of Noah (Gen. 6:9), of Shem, Ham, and Japheth (10:1), of Shem (11:10), of Terah (11:27), of Ishmael (25:12), of Isaac (25:19), of Esau (36:9), of Jacob (17:2), and finally of Aaron and Moses (Num. 3:1). Thus, the transmis-sion of the life given by God was assured up to the priests who were the descendants of Aaron, who is emphasized as much as Moses by P.

Furthermore, three covenants mark this abridged history. With Noah God sealed a covenant with all living beings. With Abra-ham the covenant was reserved for his descendants if they ob-served the Sabbath and circumcision. Finally, the third alliance made Aaron and his successors the dispensers of the divine mer-cies (Lev. 8-9). Leviticus and Numbers make up the rest of the P document.

In 538 B.C., Cyrus, king of the Persians and conqueror of Ba-bylon, authorized the deported population to go back home. Fifty thousand Jews[3] returned to Jerusalem and undertook the rebuilding of the Temple, which was inaugurated in 515 B.C. From then on, Palestine included Samaria in the north, which was inhabited by populations imported by the Assyrians, and Judea in the south, which was under the religious authority of the high priest because there was no longer any king, either in the south or the north. The Persian power left total religious autonomy to the Jews.

The priests returning from Babylon carried with them their written productions, which they imposed on the people who had stayed on the land (Ezra 7:11–26). They thereby brought about the unification of all the basic texts: J, E, D, P. Called thereafter "the Law" (Pentateuch), this was to be the charter of the Jews under Persian rule and later under the Greek and Roman rules.

THE SYSTEM OF PURITY

From that time on, until the destruction of Jerusalem in A.D. 70, Judea was under the political heel of foreign imperialism, but was to keep its religious autonomy under the power of the priestly caste. In fact, this religious power was equally political, precisely because the Jewish Law, which was recognized by the conquerors, regulated in minute detail the production, circulation, and consumption of products at the economic, political, and ideological levels (goods, people, and ideas). We shall come back to this point in the following chapter.

Now this Law, which was expressed especially in Leviticus, was characterized by the idea of *purity*. It relied on a magical conception of the universe: life and death were immutable sacred factors linked to the mysterious powers that governed the world. To obtain life (the blessing) and avoid death (the curse) could be achieved only by practices that warded off any anomaly in the order of things, that is, the healthy disposition of humans and elements established by the gods.

Piety consists of respecting the implicit and general legislation, to prevent any accident from altering the order of things. . . . The nature of religion consists of preserving it from every threat: eclipses, the birth of twins or albinos, natural wonders, sweating statues, sexual intercourse with animals, the varying (and interminable) list of taboos, and blasphemies. The equilibrium is fragile, the mechanism delicate. A prohibition violated brings on catastrophes, floods or epidemics, calamities and famine, if the priest is not there to indicate soon enough the means of repairing the offense. One must atone for the anomaly, the fault, the error, the crime, the unintended transgression (it all amounts to the same thing), in order to restore the interrupted regularity.[4]

Let us look a little more in detail at how this system functioned.

Food

Of all animals on land these are the creatures you may eat: you may eat any animal which has a parted foot or a cloven hoof and also chews the cud; those which have only a cloven hoof or only chew the cud you may not eat. These are: the camel, because it chews the cud but has not a cloven hoof; you shall regard it as unclean. . . . The pig, because it has a parted foot and a cloven hoof but does not chew the cud; you shall regard it as unclean. . . . Every creature in the water that has neither fins nor scales shall be as vermin to you. . . . Whoever touches their dead bodies [i.e., of the impure animals] shall be unclean till evening. Anything on which any of them falls when they are dead, shall be unclean, any article of wood or garment, or skin, or sacking, any article in regular use; it shall be plunged into water but shall remain unclean until evening, when it shall be clean. . . . This, then, is the law concerning beast and bird, every living creature that swims in the water and every living creature that teems on the land. It is to make a distinction between the unclean and the clean, between the living creatures that may be eaten and living creatures that may not be eaten [Lev. 11].

One understands better the rigor of these magical regulations if one remembers that what one eats to live are cadavers. Therefore, death is at the center of life, always threatening. From this comes the extreme care which had to be exercised with the laws of eating. But it was not only a question of hygiene, as has been often said. Or rather it was a magical respect for the rules of hygiene, which could maintain untouched the circular complementarity of life and death.

Family

The main prohibition was obviously that of incest of which Levi-Strauss[5] has shown the significance. By prohibiting sexual union with women relatives, it rendered necessary union with women far away and at the same time made women relatives potential wives of men from afar. Thus sexual union became the object of an exchange, and the prohibition of a nearby exchange made possible a more general exchange. But homosexuality and bestiality were also forbidden, and menstrual blood and afterbirth as well as sperm were declared unclean. Thus it seems that what must be conjured and controlled was sexual violence, which threatened to disorganize social life and work.

This is what Georges Bataille has said with regard to incest:

> Why would such a sanction be imposed with so much force—everywhere—if it were not opposed to an impulse difficult to overcome, like that of the genetic activity? . . . The relation between incest and the obsessive value of sexuality for humankind does not appear easily, but this value exists and certainly must be tied to the existence of sexual prohibitions envisaged in general.[6]

Worship

René Girard has shown admirably that the social order is an organized ensemble of differences on which the harmony and equilibrium of the community depend.[7] Not to differentiate, therefore, means violence, the breakdown of values and of hierarchies, the failure to distinguish Good and Evil. It means impurity, which can only be resolved by a purifying violence.

The means of purification was worship, and more precisely the cultic sacrifice. In sacrificing animals according to ritual, people sought to exorcise the violence within them (and among them) and to fix it on the victim, which was transformed into a scapegoat (Lev. 16).

This conception was typically religious. It presupposed a society entirely organized around rites and dependent on them to regulate its problems. Such a society was "incapable of becoming reconciled on its own face-to-face relationship of the social contract, incapable of being reconciled without victims."[8] This was, in effect, the Jewish society after the return from the Exile.

PURITY VERSUS THE GIFT:
THE LAW VERSUS THE PROPHETS

Thus the system of the gift, which was promoted by the prophetic milieus of the north (and certain Deuteronomist prophets of the south, like Jeremiah), was finally dominated by the system of purity imposed by the priestly caste of Jerusalem. This is why, in the final edition that they made of the Bible, the priests reduced the system of the gift to a code of moral precepts. This was the casuistry of which the scribes were specialists. In this way the system of the gift had been completely reversed by the priests. It had become the Law in the service of the powerful to crush the poor. The great voices of the prophets were forgotten, like the voice of Amos who cried out in the name of Yahweh:

> I hate, I spurn your pilgrim-feasts;
> I will not delight in your sacred ceremonies.
> When you present your sacrifices and offerings,
> I will not accept them,
> nor look on the buffaloes of your shared-offerings.
> Spare me the sound of your songs;
> I cannot endure the music of your lutes.
> Let justice roll on like a river
> and righteousness like an ever-flowing stream
>   [Amos 5:21–24].

Thus the powerful dynamism of the prophetic accounts from Abraham to Elijah was enclosed in cultic legalism. In that way the ideology of the dominant class finally succeeded in imposing itself.[9]

One sees a striking example in this passage of Ezekiel written during the Exile, which foresaw in detail the future reorganization of worship in the rebuilt Temple of Jerusalem:

> These are the words of the Lord God: No foreigner, uncircumcized in mind and body, shall enter my sanctuary, not even a foreigner living among the Israelites. . . . But the levitical priests . . . they shall enter my sanctuary . . . to serve me. . . . When they come to the gates of the inner court they shall dress in linen. . . . They shall wear linen turbans, and linen drawers on their loins. . . . No priest shall drink wine. . . . He may not marry a widow or a divorced woman; he may marry a virgin of Israelite birth. He may, however, marry the widow of a priest. They shall teach my people to distinguish the sacred from the profane and show them the difference between clean and unclean [Ezek. 44:9, 16–18, 22–23].

Chapter 6

Class Struggle in First-Century Palestine

After the return of the deported people from exile (538 B.C.), Palestine underwent various political situations. First it was a part of the Persian Empire. Then in 333 B.C. Alexander conquered the entire region. At his death in 323, his successors divided up his empire. Judea came under the domination of the Ptolemies of Egypt (323–197 B.C.) and then of the Seleucids of Syria (197–142 B.C.). In 167 B.C. the Maccabee brothers revolted and took power. They were the priestly and royal dynasty of the Hasmoneans. Their quarrels led the Romans to intervene. In 64 B.C. Pompey turned Syria-Palestine into a Roman province, and took Jerusalem in 63 B.C. The Hasmoneans remained chief priests and kings. In 37 B.C. Herod the Great became king of Palestine. At his death in 4 B.C. his sons split up the country: Archelaus ruled in Judea and Samaria; Herod Antipas in Galilee and Perea; Philip in Iturea and Trachonitis, and so forth. In A.D. 6 the emperor Augustus deposed Archelaus and transformed Judea-Samaria into a province with a procurator, under the direct administration of a colonial Roman functionary. From A.D. 26 to 36 this official was Pontius Pilate. This was the situation described with precision by Luke 3:1.[1]

To better understand the historical reality that characterized this geographical carving up, we turn to our analysis of the three levels—economics, politics, and ideology.

THE ECONOMIC LEVEL

The economy of Palestine in the first century of our era rested essentially on *agriculture*.[2] This represented three sources of production:

—Farming, especially in Galilee. It consisted of grains (barley and wheat) and fruits (dates, figs, grapes, and olives) from which came wine, oil, wax, honey, and perfume (the balm extracted from the trees of Jericho).

—Grazing, chiefly in Judea. It consisted of herds of small and large cattle.

—Fishing, in the lake of Tiberius.

Industry was not highly developed: there were no minerals, only stone quarries. But there were numerous *artisans* (weavers, clothmakers, tailors, blacksmiths, and carpenters) as well as large-scale public works like the construction of the Temple that employed many laborers.

Commerce was fairly limited. Palestine had no great port, and Judea was off the great trade routes. Only Galilee was open to international traffic. The merchants were mainly small shopkeepers or peddlers.

But one fundamental distinction existed between the villages and cities. The former were peopled by small farmers, some of whom worked on privately owned acreage, which was getting smaller and smaller because of the high birthrate that led to the subdivision of family property. Others worked as sharecroppers on great landholdings whose owners lived in the city. These were the great domains that regulated the rhythm of production and prices. In the cities unemployment was frequent, work unstable, and begging widespread. The case of Jerusalem was very unusual. Badly located in a dry region without communication lines, short of raw materials and water, the city sheltered a heavy population of about thirty thousand people. The population was largely made up of a large number of subproletarians, absentee landowners, and a crowd of religious functionaries employed by the Temple. The Temple was the chief source of income, thanks to the taxes and the pilgrimages, which doubled the population at the time of the Passover.

The system of taxes explains why, despite the abundance of natural resources, the peasant masses lived "in dismal poverty."[3] In fact, the Romans raised taxes equal to one forth of the harvest each year or every other year. To this was added payment in kind and forced labor to feed the occupation troops as well as numerous tolls and customs set by the publicans who took care of the collection of the taxes. Furthermore, under Jewish law each farmer had to set aside about 12 percent of what remained of the harvest for the priestly tithe and the burnt offering, plus a second tithe for the poor or as a reserve in the Temple. In addition, the sabbatical year implied the loss of at least a year and a half of agricultural products every seven years.

These excessive bleedings, along with the continued increase of prices, rendered life extremely difficult for the rural and urban laboring classes. Day laborers were reduced to poverty, and slaves from the large holdings joined the robber bands that raided the countryside. It was among them that the Zealots arose to lead a guerrilla struggle against the Romans and their collaborators, the ruling class of large landowners, high officials, and chief priests who profited to the maximum from this state of affairs.

On the economic level, therefore, we can characterize the social formation of first-century Palestine as "sub-Asian." It consisted of village communities and a temple-state, which took the surplus from the villages, and was intergrated into the Roman imperial system.

This system, furthermore, was perfectly summed up in its monetary apparatus: Jewish coins (the shekel) were used to pay the tithes, Roman coins (the denarius) were used for taxes, and Greek or Phoenician coins (the drachma or mina) were used for commerce.

THE POLITICAL LEVEL

Real power was in the hands of the Romans, but they had the custom of leaving to their provinces a rather broad internal autonomy under the procurator of Judea-Samaria.[4] Therefore, the chief priest exercised his functions in the framework of the Jewish law, and the legate of Syria oversaw Galilee only from a distance. The Romans intervened only in time of troubles, but then repression was ferocious. Two thousand persons were crucified in 4 B.C. after the first Zealot revolt that was provoked by a census of the population.

In the villages communal affairs were regulated by a council of elders, the Sanhedrin. In the cities these councils were taken over by the great landowners. In Jerusalem the Sanhedrin consisted of seventy-one members, the chief priests, elders, and scribes. It was at the same time the supreme court (criminal, political, and religious) and the seat of the government of Judea, but its ideological power extended to all of Palestine and even to the Diaspora. However independent it appeared, this apparatus of the Jewish state depended very strictly on the Romans. In effect, it was the procurator who named or deposed the chief priest, and the lands of the great property owners, the elders, belonged by law to the Romans who could expropriate them at any moment. That only gave greater importance to the scribes, whom we shall consider later. But it confirmed from the political point of view that Palestine was dominated by Rome. We shall see that Palestine's internal cohesion was assured essentially at the ideological level.

THE IDEOLOGICAL LEVEL

The ideological products of first-century Palestine have already been seen in their main lines: the Law and the Prophets whose conditions of production we have analyzed. But after the Exile other texts were produced.

Wisdom Literature

Under the Persian domination (538–333 B.C.), and later under the domination of the Ptolemies (323–197 B.C.), a certain political stability and the growing influence of Hellenism led upper-class Jews to reflect on the human condition.

The collection of Proverbs—a practical breviary of wisdom for bourgeois youth—was put together in the sixth century B.C. The book of Job in the fifth century posed like the Greek tragedies of Aeschylus and Sophocles the problem of evil and suffering, and condemned lack of moderation, which was punished by the gods. *Qoheleth*, who was called Ecclesiastes, the preacher, somewhat in the style of Epicurus (same period: fourth to third centuries B.C. invited one to taste pleasure but not to forget the obsessive presence of death. The reflections of Jesus, son of Sirach (second century B.C.), on the art of living were much more moralistic and reactionary. Thus he has received an important place from the church in its liturgy, which has given him the traditional name of Ecclesiasticus.

As for the book of the Wisdom of Solomon, which was doubtless written in Alexandria about 50 B.C. and very much inspired by the Greek philosopher Plato, it was the first in the Bible, that is in the Apocrypha, to distinguish between body and soul (9:15) and to use the word *immortality* (8:13).

The producers of these texts—the scribes about whom we shall speak later—essentially were raising questions about the destiny of the individual. The scrupulous observance of the system of purity imposed by the priestly caste did not seem to them to bring the happiness promised to the "righteous"! Influenced by Greek thought, they sought to reconcile their Yahwist faith and a day-to-day wisdom. It was the epoch, moreover, from which the current idea of philosophy dates[5],—the idea expressed in the phrase that advises people to "take things philosophically."

The Apocalypses

In the sixth century B.C. in Persia, Zarathustra had preached a new religion based on the revelation or apocalypse of a universal combat between Good and Evil, that would lead up to an eschatological last judgment, that is, a judgment at the end of time. During that judgment a redeemer would bring about the resurrection of the dead, the eternal punishment of the wicked, and the reward of the good.

This vision of a universe divided into heaven/earth/sea (the abyss) and peopled with angels and demons must have already influenced the Jews, who since their return from the Exile in the sixth century B.C. had lived under Persian domination.

But in all likelihood it was under the oppressive rule of the Seleucids (197–142 B.C.) that the first Jewish apocalypses appeared. As spokesmen for the opposition of the popular sectors to the Seleucid sovereignty and to the corrupt priestly power that supported it, the scribal authors of these texts affirmed their ferocious attachment to the traditional faith. Nourished by the ancient prophets, they rediscovered the prophets'eschatological annunciations and enlarged upon them. The Maccabean revolt (167 B.C.) showed a mentality determined to struggle against the powers of evil and to hope for a resurrection (2 Macc. 12:38–46). The same term—"abomination of desolation"—figured in 1 Maccabees 1:54 and in Daniel 9:27. The book of Daniel was the only apocalypse to appear in the Bible beside Revelation, the book attributed to St. John. But many other texts of this type were produced which one can still read today. They were generally placed under the name of great personages of the Bible: Enoch, Abraham, Jacob, Moses, Baruch, and Esdras. All these texts are characterized by a pessimistic and catastrophic vision of the world. The divine order of the universe has been shaken by the forces of evil, for example the sins of Adam, and is headed for ruin in frightful convulsions. But salvation was to come through a "Son of Man" (Dan. 7:13), sent by God to inaugurate the messianic kingdom (the Ethiopian Enoch 2:13–16), which recovered the Jewish expectation of a descendant of David who has been royally "anointed" (the meaning of Messiah) and who was to restore the kingdom to Israel.[6]

The Rabbinic Literature

The people deported to Babylon gradually had forgotten Hebrew and spoke Aramaic, the language of their conquerors. In the synagogues a rabbi—the word means "teacher" or "doctor"—translated the scriptures, once they had been read in Hebrew. These translations sometimes were transformed into paraphrases and interpretations. Finally, all that was also fixed by writing in what is called the *Targum*. It enables one to know how the rabbis, the doctors of the Law, read the scriptures.

On the other hand, the teachings, commentaries, and injunctions of the rabbis made up the *Talmud*, whose production was to continue until the fifth century after Christ.[7]

The Scribes

The Persian, Greek (except the Seleucids), and Roman conquerors always left to the Jews freedom of religion. Therefore,

during and after the Exile the priestly caste (a closed caste reserved only to the supposed legitimate descendants of Aaron)
took on more and more importance. We have seen that it succeeded in imposing on the people the system of purity and of prac-
tically eliminating the prophetic current. Little by little, the chief
priest became the real chief of the Jews, just as the Temple became the center of Israel.

However, the priestly preponderance was taken over bit by bit.
First, because the Romans after the time of Herod the Great
named and replaced the chief priests at will, and, second, because
a new class progressively gained influence: the scribes, rabbis,
and doctors of the Law.

Undoubtedly born in exile out of the necessity to translate and
interpret the scriptures (see Nehemiah 8), the scribes had become
real specialists. As jurists and ethicists, they elucidated the Law
and prescribed its practice (see the *Targum*). They had opened
schools and lived surrounded by disciples. It was they who led the
worship in the synagogues. Some were priests, but the majority
lived off a small trade or offerings. Linked to the dominant class
by their functions, they were often ideologically opposed to it.[8]

The Pharisees

During the revolt of the Maccabees (167 B.C.) a group of pious
Jews came together—"stalwarts of Israel, every one of them a
volunteer in the cause of the Law" (1 Macc. 2:42). Gathered in
communities, they scrupulously observed the precepts of the system of purity and prepared themselves by prayer and fasting for
the great divine intervention which they awaited. They were called
Pharisees, which means the "separated ones." As extreme na-
tionalists, who were hostile to the foreign conquerors, they none-
theless did not seek to bring about political change by force. They
looked forward to the arrival of the Messiah and believed in resurrection. Their prestige among the people was considerable. Many
scribes belonged to pharisaic communities.

The Sadducees

In opposition to the Pharisees, the Sadducees, who derived
their name from Zadok, a chief priest in the period of Solomon

(1 Kings 2:35), were recruited among the priestly aristocracy and the wealthy families of Jerusalem. Politically they collaborated with the Roman occupation; they were first of all concerned for public order. Religiously very conservative, they held to the ancient Law and repudiated more recent beliefs in angels, demons, the coming kingdom, and the resurrection.

The Essenes

No text of the Bible speaks of the Essenes. They are known only by a few pages of Flavius Josephus and Philo of Alexandria, and especially by the documents discovered since A.D. 1947 at Qumran near the Dead Sea. Living in monastic communities that had a novitiate, obligatory celibacy, the community of goods, and a strict discipline, they challenged the legitimacy of the chief priests, kept away from the Temple, and observed their own calendar. Being a sect of the "pure" and very much influenced by the Persian apocalypse, they despised the body and believed in angels and demons. Believing themselves to be the true people of God, they waited for the coming of the Messiah.

The Zealots

The Bible also says nothing about the Zealots of whom Flavius Josephus speaks. The first manifestation of this sect seems to have been the insurrection led by Judas the Galilean (see Acts 5:37) against the census undertaken by the Romans at the death of Herod the Great (4 B.C.). Recruiting among the most oppressed of the proletariat, crushed by a pitiless system of taxation, very religious and ultranationalist, they were in a way the activists of Pharisaism. They wanted to chase out the pagan occupation and reestablish a theocracy; this was what makes them "reactionaries" seeking to restore the sub-Asian condition in its purity. But unable to confront the Roman army directly, they organized commando operations or took advantage of large gatherings, such as Passover in Jerusalem, to stab soldiers and collaborators. From this custom was derived their other name, Sicarii, from *sica* meaning "dagger." The Gospel of Mark explicitly names a Zealot among the twelve who followed Jesus—Simon the Zealot (Mark

3:19). Oscar Cullmann has shown that Judas Iscariot could signify "the Sicarius," and that Simon Barjona, the name of Simon Peter, according to John 1:42, doubtless means "terrorist."[9]

In A.D. 66 the procurator Florus took from the treasury of the Temple seventeen talents of gold, which amounted to about $5 million. [10] The people of Jerusalem rebelled, massacred a Roman garrison, and took over the city. The chief priest was killed, and another was chosen by lot from among the legitimate families. The fiscal archives or certificates of debt were destroyed. All through the country Zealots organized the resistance. It took four years for the Romans to regain their hold. In September A.D.70 after a terrible six-month's siege, Titus, son of the emperor Vespasian, overcame the last defenders of Jerusalem, razed the city, and led the Zealot chiefs to Rome for his triumphal march.[11]

A SOCIAL FORMATION OF CLASSES

In short, first-century Palestine was a class-structured society at every level. At the economic level the masses were fiercely exploited by the privileged. In politics the priestly class supported by the great landowners held the mechanism of the state in their hands. Ideologically the ruling class imposed its ideology (essentially the system of purity), which was passed on in diverse ways by the groups, sects, and parties.

Over all that lay the shadow of Rome, which predetermined the social formation at the two first levels by taxation and military occupation.

And the role of the Temple at Jerusalem stood out clearly. It was a treasury of public finances, the seat of the Sanhedrin, and a holy place *par excellence*. Horizontally, it was the center of the world, the maximum concentration of purity and holiness; vertically, it was the axis of the world because heaven touched earth there. It was the symbol of the entire social formation. That is why its destruction by Titus in A.D. 70 symbolized for Jews and for Christians the collapse of Judaism.

Part II

The Gospel According to St. Mark,
or a Narration of the Practice
of Jesus

Chapter 7

Christians at Rome in A.D. 71

We are getting ready to read the Gospel according to St. Mark in terms of its conditions of production. We have the working hypothesis, which is to be verified (see p. 62), that this text was written in Rome very soon after the destruction of Jerusalem by Titus (A.D. 70) or about the year 71. Thus we shall take a look at Rome at that time.

Let us recall first of all some names briefly to situate the period. After the reign of Nero (A.D. 54–68), which ended tragically, a pitiless civil war was waged among three candidates for emperor. A fourth candidate, Vespasian, won and reigned for ten years (A.D. 69–79). His two sons were to succeed him: Titus (A.D. 79–81), and then Domitian (A.D. 81–96).

ROME IN A.D. 71

The Roman Empire was then at its peak.[1] Since the fourth century B.C., the city of Rome had gradually conquered all of Italy, then the whole of the Mediterranean basin (*mare nostrum*). This implacable expansionism profoundly modified not only the conquered countries but Rome itself. We shall analyze the Roman social formation at the economic, political, and ideological levels.

Economy

All these conquests had for their purpose and consequence to drain immense riches toward Rome—the fruits of pillage, taxes and charges, and the methodical exploitation of the occupied ter-

53

ritories. A Greek writer of the first century A.D., Aelius Aristides, expressed this gigantic effort of bloodshed in the following way:

> From the far corners of the earth and the seas flow toward you the products of all the seasons and of all countries, those of the rivers and lakes, and all that is born of the labor of Greeks and barbarians. . . . So many transport vessels come to unload on the banks of the Tiber that Rome is a kind of universal market for the world. The fruits of India and of Arabia, . . . the tissues of Babylon, the jewels of furthest Barbary arrive in Rome in great quantity and with great ease.[2]

Thus the colonial governors, business leaders, merchants, and shipbuilders enriched themselves. On the reverse side, the conquered peoples were fiercely exploited, as we shall see for Palestine, and the small rural Italian farmers were ruined by the massive importation. (Wine from Gaul, for example, had to be controlled in order not to compete too much with Italian wine.)[3] The result was a rise in prices, inflation, and a devaluation of the money during the rule of under Nero.

But the principal characteristic of this imperial system was the fact that it rested on slavery.[4] Prisoners of war, indebted peasants, populations rounded up and sold on the block, and slaves represented the chief instrument of labor. Unpaid, they were considered by Roman law as merchandise and unmercifully exploited. They were the basis of the economy. In a city like Rome, which probably had a million inhabitants under Vespasian, they made up about half of the population. In the countryside they were the main laborers on the large properties (*latifundia*) belonging to the patrician families that little by little had dispossessed the small farmers of their lands. This was graphically shown by Appian, a Greek historian of the second century after Christ:

> The rich, after having taken over the largest part of these nonassigned lands (from the *ager publicus*), were confident after a time that no one would ever take them away from them. They then turned toward the small neighboring prop-

erties owned by the poor and, seizing them, either nicely by purchase or by force, had them cultivated from then on not as simple fields but as great estates. To increase their value, they used slaves as farmers and shepherds, for fear that if they used freemen they would see them taken away from cultivation to military service [which lasted twenty years!] What is more, this procedure brought them considerable income through the birth of slaves. . . . Thus they amassed great wealth, and the number of slaves multiplied in the country. The Italians, on the other hand, suffered depopulation and shortage of men, exhausted as they were by poverty, taxation, and military service. If there was sometimes a little relaxation of these evils, then the Italians were corrupted by laziness, because the land was in the hands of the rich and they employed as cultivators only slaves in the place of freemen.[5]

This text shows clearly the consequences of the system of slavery. Free and easily renewable, it put a brake on the surge of productive forces (there was to be no important technological progress under the Roman Empire), and it ruined the small producers.

The depopulation of the countryside reinforced the process of urbanization led by Roman politics, which resulted in the organization of municipalities. Hundreds of thousands of the unemployed converged on Rome, and to them the emperors distributed grain and money so that they could be entertained by the fights of gladiators and the chariot races. Hence the saying *panem et circenses* or "bread and games."

Rome was overpopulated, unhealthy, and subject to frequent and irresistible fires.[6] (There were twelve fires in six years, including the one of A.D. 64 under Nero that destroyed ten of the fourteen city zones.) Known as Urbis (the city), Rome was a good symbol of the empire. It contained palaces of indescribable luxury, squalid neighborhoods, and a cosmopolitan population from all over the known world. It was a parasite sucking up the riches of the universe without being able to give work to its own children. In Rome were concentrated all the contradictions of an imperial system of slave labor. And it was from this that Rome was to die, as the book of Revelation (Apocalypse)—attributed to the apostle John and written about the time of—Domitian seems to predict:

> "Alas, alas for the great city, the mighty city of Babylon! In a single hour your doom has struck!" The merchants of the earth . . . will weep and mourn for her because no one any longer buys their cargoes, cargoes of gold and silver, jewels and pearls, cloths of purple and scarlet, silks and fine linens; all kinds of scented woods, ivories, and every sort of thing made of costly woods, bronze, iron, or marble; cinnamon and spice, incense, perfumes and frankincense; wine, oil, flour and wheat, sheep and cattle, horses, chariots, slaves, and the lives of men [Rev. 18:10–13].

Politics

The Roman Empire was, in fact, a military dictatorship. Supported by the army, the emperor (the commander-in-chief) took on all the powers shared up to then between the senate (representing *latifundista* patrician families) and the people (representing the Roman citizens). He encouraged more and more the development of a business bourgeoisie, the knights,[7] who occupied the higher functions of the administration and participated directly in the imperialist exploitation through the great colonial trade and through the furnishing of military supplies.[8]

In this social formation the state was a power of coercion benefiting the ruling class of landowners who were deprived of the means of production. But in a way the state tended to develop for itself: an imperial bureaucracy grew up under the direction of freed imperial slaves. (Narcissus, a freedman of the emperor Claudius, directed the foreign relations service.) Gradually the bureaucracy took away all the power of the deliberating assemblies, especially of the senate. The public treasury (*aerarium*) was neglected in favor of the Emperor's treasury (*fiscus*). The emperor was the greatest landholder and handled all the public expenditures.[9]

Thus power was shot through with contradictions that continued to grow: the emperor-state relied on the knights, the army, and the people in bringing down the old ruling class, the senatorial nobility. The city of Rome, which was the seat of power and the center of the empire, was more and more dependent economically on the provinces. Thus the centrifugal movements of revolt were characteristic. Often military mutinies made and unmade emperors. And the provinces rose up one after the other. In the time of Vespasian, Gaul had the rebellion of Civilis and the prophetess Velleda,[10] and Palestine had the rebellion of the Zealots.

Ideology

The ideology[11] of the ruling class was obviously very much affected by this situation of crisis. The nobles, deprived of power, withdrew into luxury and debauchery, or pessimism and cynicism (see the disillusioned reflections of Seneca, the satirical works of Marcial and Juvenal, and the *Satiricon* of Petronius). Furthermore, the old Roman religion became increasingly diluted in the great ideological and ethnic trappings of the empire. In this sort of void the religions coming from the East had much success: small circles, evermore numerous, were initiated into the mysteries of the next world.

As for the oppressed classes of ruined peasants, citizens, the unemployed, the wanderers, foreigners, and slaves, they had no earthly hope and, as Engels said, "The lost paradise is behind them." They had no way to express themselves. Phaedrus, the author of fables that served as models for La Fontaine (for example, "The Wolf and the Lamb") tried to speak of the distress of the little people, but was suppressed. As a result the Eastern religions, which were imported notably by merchants and soldiers, developed. They promised salvation and immortality and presented the face of a suffering and resurrected god such as Attis or Mithra whose image was tender toward all those unfortunates.

THE CHRISTIAN COMMUNITY

This was the Rome where some Christians were living about the year 71. How long had they been there? We do not know exactly, but the historian Suetonius writes: "[In 49], the emperor Claudius expelled from Rome the Jews who acted under the influence of Chrestus."[12] We can suppose that these were Christians converted from Judaism, and that Chrestus meant "Christus." Moreover, the Acts of the Apostles indicates this expulsion (18:2). Furthermore, very likely in 58, Paul addressed a long letter "to all the beloved of God who are at Rome" (Rom. 1:7). And we know for a fact that there were Christians at Rome in the time of Nero because the historian Tacitus says that Nero made them bear the responsibility for the fire of 64, which the crowd blamed on him:

> In order, if possible, to remove the imputation [that Nero had started the fire], he determined to transfer the guilt to others. For this purpose he punished, with exquisite torture, a race of men detested for their evil practices, by vulgar appellation commonly called Christians.
>
> The name was derived from Christ, who in the reign of Tiberius, suffered under Pontius Pilate, the procurator of Judaea. By that event the sect, of which he was the founder, received a blow, which, for a time, checked the growth of a dangerous superstition; but it revived soon after, and spread with recruited vigour, not only in Judaea, the soil that gave it birth, but even in the city of Rome, the common sink into which everything infamous and abominable flows like a torrent from all quarters of the world. Nero proceeded with his usual artifice. He found a set of profligate and abandoned wretches, who were induced to confess themselves guilty, and, on the evidence of such men, a number of Christians were convicted, not indeed, upon clear evidence of their having set the city on fire, but rather on account of their sullen hatred of the whole human race. They were put to death with exquisite cruelty, and to their sufferings Nero added mockery and derision. Some were covered with the skins of wild beasts, and left to be devoured by dogs; others were nailed to the cross; numbers were burnt alive; and many, covered over with inflammable matter, were lighted up, when the day declined, to serve as torches during the night.
>
> For the convenience of seeing this tragic spectacle, the emperor lent his own gardens. He added the sports of the circus, and assisted in person, sometimes driving a curricle,

and occasionally mixing with the rabble in his coachman's dress. At length the cruelty of these proceedings filled every breast with compassion. Humanity relented in favour of the Christians. The manners of that people were, no doubt, of a pernicious tendency, and their crimes called for the hand of justice: but it was evident, that they fell a sacrifice, not for the public good, but to glut the rage and cruelty of one man only.[13]

Who were these Christians? The end of the Letter of Paul to the Romans, the authenticity of which has been questioned, includes twenty-four names of persons whom the apostle wished to greet personally. From the names one can see that some were Greeks (Apelles, Epaenetus, Tryphaena, and Tryphosa); others were Romans (Julia, Urban, Rufus, who was perhaps the son of Simon the Cyrenean, see Mark 15:21); others were Jews (Andronicus, Aquila, Aristobulus, Junias, Mary, and Prisca). It seems also that some were names of slaves or freedmen (Ampliatus, Asyncritus, Hermas, Nereus, Olympas, Patrobas, Persis, Philologus, Phlegon, Stachys).[14] Finally, mention of "those of the house of Narcissus" indicates that there were Christians in the entourage of the famous freedman who had become secretary of foreign affairs and about whom Racine wrote in *Britannicus*.

In addition, during his captivity in Rome (61–63), Paul wrote especially to the Colossians, giving the names of even more Christians at Rome: Aristarchus, Mark (the author of the Gospel?), and Demas (Col. 4:10 ff.).

In other letters Paul mentioned other Christians living in Rome: "those who belong to the imperial establishment" (Phil. 4:22); "Eubulus, Pudens, Linus, Claudia, and all the brotherhood" (2 Tim. 4:21).

Finally, we read in the Acts of the Apostles that at his arrival as a prisoner in Italy, Paul found brethren at the port of Puteoli, near Naples (Acts. 28:14) and at Rome: "The Christians there had had news of us and came out to meet us as far as Appii Forum and Tres Tabernae" (28:15).

To sum up, these lists of names do not tell us much except that in the time of Vespasian there must have been in Rome a group of Christians already large and from very diverse origins, probably from the lower social classes. However, the nephew of Vespasian, Flavius Clemens, and his wife, Flavia Domitilla, were evidently Christians. Domitian had the husband executed and exiled the wife; one of the first catacombs still bears her name.[15]

The letter of Paul to the Romans certainly seems to indicate that the people who received it were not, at least in the majority, of Jewish origin: "I have something to say to you Gentiles" (11:13). But until 70, Christians were often confused with Jews, as the above quotation from Suetonius shows.[16] And the link remained very strong with Judaism, as the Epistle to the Romans precisely shows:

> But if some of the branches have been lopped off, and you, a wild olive, have been grafted in among them, and have come to share the same root and sap as the olive, do not make yourselves superior to the branches. If you do so, remember that it is not you who sustain the root: the root sustains you [Rom. 11:17-18].

Furthermore, the Acts of the Apostles testifies that Jerusalem remained the capital of the Christians, probably until its destruction in A.D. 70. We shall see the importance of this remark for the understanding of the Gospel of Mark.

As far as the *organization* of the Christian community is concerned, our information comes essentially from the Acts of the Apostles and the letters of Paul.[17] We might assume, in fact, that, like the other communities, the one at Rome was presided over by elders, that is, presbyters (from which the word *priest* comes). The bishops, —that is, episcopes or overseers—seem to have been responsible first of all to manage the materials and to assure certain services (*diakonia*) with the deacons. This signifies undoubtedly that the list, which was established in the second century, of popes or bishops of Rome as successors to Peter has little chance of reflecting reality. According to this list, Linus was supposed to have filled this charge from 68 to 80.

What is certain is that the Christians did not yet have official places of worship and gathered in people's homes. They had a meal together (the eucharistic ritual was not yet fixed) and read a passage of their scriptures, letters of apostles such as Paul, or collections of stories about Jesus or of Jesus' sayings. These stories and sayings were collected prior to the editing of the Gospels. An example is found in the letter Clement, the bishop of Rome, wrote to the Corinthians in A.D. 96. He quoted some "words of the Lord Jesus" which do not appear in any of the texts of the New Testament (1 Clement 13:1-2; 46:8). It seems that an impatient, eschatological expectation marked this first Christian generation: "For deliverance is nearer to us now than it was when first we believed" (Rom. 13:11; cf. 2 Thess. 2:10). We shall see that the Gospel of Mark testifies to the disappointment of that hope.

Finally, we must remember the climate of repression and insecurity of the Christians at Rome. After the expulsion in A.D. 49, and after the persecution by Nero in 64 (when tradition says that Peter and Paul perished), the Christians had to hide, to be wary of informers officially employed by the imperial administration, and to punish traitors. The Gospel of Mark bears the trace of this also.

THE TEXT OF MARK

What is known about this text?

A bishop at the beginning of the second century named Papias made this statement: "Mark, who was an interpreter for Peter, wrote exactly, but not in order, all that he remembered of the words or actions of the Lord."[18] Other witnesses of the second and third centuries also attributed this text to Mark.

Who was Mark? The Acts of the Apostles speak of a certain "John surnamed Mark" (12:12) whose mother's house served as a refuge for Peter at Jerusalem. He was taken by Barnabas, his cousin (Col. 4:10), and by Paul to Antioch (Acts 12:25). He followed Paul during his first journey (13:5); then he accompanied Barnabas to Cyprus (15:37-39). Was this the same person of whom Paul spoke in his letters as being at Rome (Col. 4:10; Phil. 24; 2 Tim. 4:11)? The first letter of Peter (5:13) also spoke of "Mark, my son."

But it is fairly probable that the Gospel of Mark is a pseudepigraphy, that is to say, a text *attributed* to a famous person. In fact, this is the case for numerous biblical books.

In any case it seems likely that this text was written for (and undoubtedly in) a Roman milieu. To be sure, it was written in Greek, but that was the second official language of the empire (the foreign service had a Latin bureau and a Greek bureau), and it was spoken fluently in the whole eastern part of the Mediterranean basin. We know, moreover, that the liturgical language of the Christians until the third century was Greek. But the Greek of Mark is very special. First of all, it is a very common type of language, with a limited but always concrete vocabulary, with a stilted syntax, and often marked by Semitic expressions. But interestingly enough, all the typically Jewish expressions are translated for readers who are ignorant of their meaning: *boanerges*, 3:17; *talitha kum*, 5:41; *corban*, 7:11; *epphata*, 7:34, *abba*, 14:36; *eli*, 15:34.

What is more, a number of words are expressly Roman: centurion, 15:39, 44, 45; legion, 5:9, 15; speculator (soldier of the guard), 6:27; denarius, 6:37; 12:15; 14:5; farthing, 12:42; praetorium, 15:16; cohort, 15:16.

In short, one has the impression in reading the Greek text of Mark of hearing a Jew speak who has difficulty expressing himself in Greek and who must take account of the fact that his readers are Romans.

It is a little as if today we heard a Palestinian speaking French to foreign workers from Portugal, Senegal, and Turkey, explaining the meaning of the words, situating the place names, and so forth.

As for the date of A.D. 71, it is our reading of Mark that justifies it. Let us say simply for the moment that we accept the position of S.G.F. Brandon:

> The second Gospel must have been composed during the years that immediately followed the sack of Jerusalem, in other words in 71 or 72, probably in the immediate context of the crushing triumph of Vespasian and Titus at Rome in 71.[19]

Chapter 8

The Narration of a Practice

The current Catholic editions of the Bible[1] split the Gospel according to St. Mark into five major parts: 1. the preparation of the ministry of Jesus; 2. the ministry of Jesus in Galilee; 3. journeys of Jesus beyond Galilee; 4. the ministry of Jesus in Jerusalem; 5. the passion and resurrection of Jesus. And subheadings further divide the text into pericopes or sections. However, we note that on one hand the large headings use the word "ministry" three times, which is very characteristic of the clergy, and on the other hand the subtitles often use the terms "preaching," "teaching," or "discourse."

This way of presenting the text of Mark to modern readers runs the risk of denaturing its role, we believe.

NARRATION/DISCOURSE

It seems to us, in fact, that Mark (we shall use this word from now on to speak of the text written by Mark) is much more a *narration* than a *discourse.*

This distinction has been proposed by contemporary linguistics for analyzing the different kinds of textual productions. A discourse is characterized by the system of the person (I-you, here-now, and demonstratives) and by verbs in all tenses except the aorist (our past tense). A narration is characterized by the system of the nonperson (absence of I-you, presence of "he") and by verbs especially in the aorist but never in the present, past, perfect, or future. This is because the narration or narrative text tells about a *practice*:

No one speaks; events (practices) seem to tell about them-selves. The fundamental tense is the aorist, which is the time of the event apart from the person of the narrator.[2]

We have seen that the current editions of the Bible freely use a heading about the "ministry" of Jesus. The text itself speaks on several occasions of his "teaching" (Mark 1:21, 22, 27) and of his "preaching" (Mark 1:38-39), and it emphasizes that the crowds were greatly amazed (Mark 1:22-27).

But oddly enough, Mark does not specify what this teaching consisted of. Why not? One sentence can enlighten us: "Many people, learning all that he [Jesus] did, came to him" (3:8). What attracted the crowds was not a teaching in the form of a discourse, but the *narration* told by a thousand voices of what Jesus *did, of his practice*.

A detail of translation allows us to verify this interpretation. In Mark 1:45, the cured leper "went out and made the whole story public; he spread it far and wide." The context obliges us to un-derstand that the story in question is what had just happened to the leper, his healing by Jesus; therefore the story is of the *practice* of Jesus toward the leper.

Now the same word *logos* or "story" is used in Mark 4:14 to explain the parable called the "sower" (about which we shall speak in chapter 12): "The seed is the word [*logos*]." That means, in our opinion, that the logos in question, sown in different soil, is indeed the story spread by the leper and all the others. It is the telling of the practice of Jesus ("all that he did," according to Mark 3:8), spreading like concentric circles around his person. And what is, therefore, the Gospel of Mark if not the textual form of this (good) news, the writing down of this energizing narration, which makes the people come out of their houses (3:7-8) and of themselves (1:12)?

A TEXT AND THE READING OF IT

Before studying the function of the narration of Mark, we must specify what a *text* and its *reading* are.

A text is a product, the result of work. The means of this pro-duction are the signs of language (pictographic, ideographic, syl-labic, and alphabetical). Modern linguistics defines a language as

a system of signs (where each sign takes its value only in oppositional relation to the whole).[3] A sign is constituted by the association of an acoustical image and of a concept, called respectively
"signifier" and "signified." The relationship of signification is
the relationship between signifier and signified: Sr/Sd. Consequently, we will not say that the signifier translates or transmits
the signified, but rather that the meaning is the product of the
relationship Sr/Sd. But just as in economic exchanges the work of
production is forgotten little by little in exalting the exchange
value of the merchandise, in the same way in ideological exchanges the work of production is obscured in the preference for
meaning.

In following the analyses of Jean-Joseph Goux[4] it is possible to
compare the evolution of economic exchanges according to
Marx—the genesis of the money form—and that of ideological
exchanges through writing:

1. The value of the use of objects.

1. Free play of signifiers (painting, poetry, etc.).

2. One merchandise is substituted for another (barter).

2. A material signifier (a sketch) is substituted for each thing (picto-graphy).

3. One merchandise is substituted for all others.

3. A signifier is substi-tuted for many things by a system of equiva-lences (ideography).

4. A merchandise with-drawn from the ex-change serves as a general equivalent in which is expressed the *value* of all the mer-chandise.

4. A restricted number of signifiers, designat-ing only sounds (sylla-bic writing), expresses the *meaning* of all things.

5. Gold, a universal general equivalent, appears as the very sign of the value.

5. Linguistic signs ap-pear as the very signs of meaning (alpha-betical writing).

Thus the invention of syllabic writing permits the lifting up of a general equivalent that regulates the circulation of signs: it is the logos, the discourse about the real, which superposes itself on the real and ends up by appearing more true than the real. This stage corresponds, on the economic level, to the appearance of money, the general equivalent that regulates economic exchanges—shekels by the royal standard of David. On the political level we have the birth of the kingdom, which was the general equivalent for political exchanges. This stage can be either theocentric dominant with the general equivalent a god, or logocentric with the general equivalent a logos, reason, or discourse.

Thus at the economic level the *value* of exchange attributed to an object is substituted in fact for the object, becoming its "double" by a "ghost" effect. For example, a consumer buys an object *as if* the price were the value in itself of the object. But Marx shows precisely that under this double, this "fetish," is hidden a secret—the true value of the merchandise, which is the time of work necessary to produce it.

In the same way, on the ideological level the *meaning* attributed to a text becomes a phantom double. The reader reads the text as if its value consisted of transmitting a reality directly when, in fact, behind this fetish is hidden a secret: the true value of a text is the work expressed in the relation Sr/Sd. "The meaning does not transcend the signs that manifest it. It does not relate to a referent as such (the thing itself in its natural existence), but to other signs, to the writing of total social signs."[5]

THE WEAVING OF CODES

Thus a text is never merely what we believe at first view—a direct message to decipher. We often imagine that authors know what they mean, choose the words, make sentences of them, and express thereby the meaning that they want to transmit. The reader, on the other hand, has only to follow the reverse procedure: in going from the form to the substance, from the container to the content, from the signifier to the signified. It is not that simple! A text is always just a part of the outpouring of words, writings, and the unsaid, which constitute the great text of the world since the world began. Authors never do more than pick up a few threads of this immense loom to weave their part according to an outline that is received more or less from the society in which they live.

Comparing the process of writing to the work of weaving, Barthes calls each thread a *code*, and the whole of the codes the braid or the weave, through which little by little is composed the tissue or the text (textile and texture are the same thing).[6] And in a text, each thread or code is known by the fact that it gathers up the relations, the linkages, the references to other texts or other places in the text—what linguist call connotations. Each of the codes produces meaning, therefore, by intercourse with all the meanings that are brought about by words and sentences. Thus "to interpret a text is not to give a meaning (more or less established, more or less free); on the contrary, it is to perceive from what plural it is made."[7]

And as Barthes points out, just as in the *Arabian Nights* a story of Scheherazade is worth a day of life, so is every narration worth ✻ an exchange:

> One does not tell a story to "entertain," to "instruct" or to satisfy a certain anthropological exercise of meaning; one narrates to obtain something in exchange. And it is this exchange that is outlined in the narration itself.[8]

Thus in the story of the succession of David, we have seen that the meaning is reduced to this: Solomon is the legitimate successor of David. But what the story does is to lead the reader to take this version of the events for the only valid one. Thus the author exchanges his narrative for the submission of the reader to Solomon's royalty.

But the reading that is interested only in the meaning is idealist, believing in the innocence and transparency of the text. The exchange is governed here by the general equivalent—just as on the economic level, fascinated by the signifier "gold," workers are unable to see the real process of production; and just as on the political level, fascinated and intimidated by power and its signifiers such as king and Caesar, the subjects find the established order natural. So on the ideological level, fascinated by a "god" or the "truth" and by the false evidence of the signified (the meaning of a text), people read with the eyes of faith and "good sense."

This is why we must bring in *materialist readings*. And this consists first of all, as we have seen it in the story of the succession of David, in looking for the set of codes and not the plan of the story, as the splitting up of our current Bible does. It is a question of:

> taking the pains (that is, the time and patience) to backtrack the tributaries of the meaning, to leave no place of the signifier without locating the code or codes for which this place is perhaps the point of departure (or arrival).[9]

For as Barthes goes on to point out:

> The text, in its wholeness, is comparable to the heavens, flat and deep at the same time, slick, without borders or fixed points. As the augur shapes an imaginary rectangle with the tip of his pointer in order to discuss certain principles of the flight of birds, the commentator traces throughout the text zones of reading, in order to observe there the migration of meanings, the outcropping of codes, the series of citations.[10]

That consists, then, of considering the text as a product and a production, and of always seeking out the work that produced it and the conditions of production that rendered it possible and necessary.

It consists, finally, in making a subversive reading that avoids the idealist fascination. It is even especially necessary since the text of Mark is, as we shall see, the subversive narration of a subversive practice. But as we shall also see, it was very quickly (and in the process of being written) taken over by the dominant ideology. It is necessary for us to take into hand once more a reading governed for centuries by all the orthodoxies and to make the subversive dynamism of Mark appear. In other words, it is necessary to see how this narration of the practice of Jesus has brought about and continues to bring about the subversion of dominant codes everywhere.

Chapter 9

An Open Narrative:
Mythology and History

A PROLOGUE IN MYTHOLOGICAL CODE

The text of Mark opens with these words: "Here begins the
Gospel of Jesus Christ the Son of God." That is to say, as we have
seen in the foregoing chapter, "Here begins the (fortunate and
energizing) narration of the (messianic) practice of Jesus."

The word *begins* is important. It indicates first of all that something is going to unfold. In fact, a beginning presupposes and
points to a continuity. The practice of Jesus therefore will be narrated according to the main law of narratives: the succession of
one thing after another in *time*. But a beginning also implies an
end. As bizarre as it might seem, Mark will not have an ending.

In effect, taking a cue from all the modern exegetes (see the
note in the Jerusalem Bible), we close the text of Mark at 16:8:
"they [the women] said nothing to anybody, for they were
afraid." What follows is certainly not from the same author.
Now this last sentence is not a closing and that is why some editions put three periods . . . after "afraid." Thus the text of Mark
is unfinished; it remains open. We are going to look for what it is
open to and why.

Right after the first sentence of the Gospel, which serves as a
heading, Mark begins a very particular kind of preamble (1:2–
15). Within the preamble there are four sequences which the Jeru-

salem Bible entitles: "The preaching of John the Baptist"; "Jesus is baptized"; "Temptation in the wilderness"; and "Jesus begins to preach."

If we remember the distinction between narration and discourse, we shall note that this preamble is a *discourse*, that is, a system of the I-you person. Here are some examples: "Here is my herald whom I send on ahead of you" (1:2); "I am not fit to unfasten his shoes" (1:8); "I have baptized you with water" (1:8); "thou art my Son, my Beloved; on thee my favour rests" (1:11). We note also the exclusion of the aorist tense with the exception of the phrases "John the Baptist appeared" (1:4) and "Jesus came" (1:9). In addition, this whole passage comes from a *code* or system of connotations or references which is to be called "mythological." We note the strangeness of the person of John the Baptist, who is living in the wilderness, clothed with camel skin, and especially do we note the presence of the schema heaven/earth/river (=hell) with the Spirit, angels, and Satan.

Now this prologue of Mark resembles strangely what the priests of the Exile gave to the books of the Law (the Pentateuch), namely, the first chapter of Genesis or the "seven days of creation." This passage is typically mythological in that it claims to tell of an event which, by definition, no one could have witnessed. It is thus a narration of what cannot be narrated, of what is situated before all science and all human memory—the foundation story of everything that followed.

As Paul Beauchamp has shown, the first chapter of Genesis presents the origins of the universe as a process of separation, that is to say, as differentiation: the primordial chaos becomes orderly in heaven, earth, and the sea.[1] We remind the reader that we presented the Priestly document and the system of purity as developments essentially intended to avoid the erasing of the differences on which the social and natural order is founded as well as to urge against the return of the leveling violence. Genesis 1 establishes, therefore, against the nondifferentiating effects of death the possibility of a cosmos or harmonious universe that facilitates the dawn of vegetation, animals, and human life. In doing so it suspends timelessness—the absence of time that is characteristic of mythologies—and inaugurates the time of history. Consequently, it also inaugurates the possibility of narratives.

The presence of this mythological prologue at the beginning of Mark shows the conditions of production of this text. More exactly, it shows the textual work that produced it. In fact, every narrative, as we have said, rests on the principle of successiveness, which is to say that it rests on historical time. But one must specify that this time is not "real time." It is a textual construction, a literary representation. Just as a painter, to give the illusion of perspective, paints lines fleeing toward the horizon, a writer, to give the illusion of what has been experienced, of the past, of what has happened, must fix in the enormous depth of time a point of departure to start off his or her narrative. For that, the procedures of the ancient writers were not the same as those of modern ones. Thus Stendhal begins *La Chartreuse de Parme* (The Charterhouse of Parma) with the words: "On 15 May, 1796 General Bonaparte made his entry into Milan. . . ." It is therefore a precisely dated event that launches the story. But the Gospel of Matthew uses a genealogical list to link the story of Jesus to a fixed, legendary personage, Abraham. Likewise, Mark opens his narrative by a prologue that places it solidly between heaven and the abyss, between the beginning and the end of time.

AN UNFINISHED STORY

This prologue of Mark is in the mythological key (as we say in music) or in a code, which is a linguistic term. The narrative of the practice of Jesus is therefore posed, or one might say programmed, by this opening. We might expect consequently that it would end in the same tonality or in the same code. Just as through the vertical mythology of heaven/earth/sea the heavenly voice and the Spirit-dove *descend* toward Jesus, who was immersed in the waters of the Jordan, in the same way the end of Mark should present an "ascension," in which Jesus *returns* from the earth toward heaven. But it does not happen, as we have seen, since Mark terminates with the suspended report of the fear of the women at the tomb. But the readers of Mark are alerted, in fact, to this incongruity, and that is why someone added verses 16:9–20, which tell of Jesus' ascension.

But whoever ended Mark in this way did not understand the structural dynamics. If the narration of the ministry of Jesus remains open, this was not by chance or by oversight.[2] It is because, as we shall see, after the death of Jesus and his bodily absence from the midst of his disciples, his presence remains under another form, and the story of his practice is continued through the stories of the practices of all Christians. In the same way the Gospel of Luke is continued in the Acts of the Apostles.

A WORK OF DEMYTHOLOGIZING

Beginning with a mythological code, the Gospel of Mark demythologizes itself. And of that we have an indication even in the prologue. In fact, the quotation from Isaiah 40:3, which immediately follows the title and introduces the appearance of John the Baptist, is truly remarkable: "A voice crying aloud in the wilderness, 'Prepare a way for the Lord; clear a straight path for him.' " To fully understand its importance, we must also read the following verse from Isaiah: "Every valley shall be lifted up, every mountain and hill brought down, rugged places shall be made smooth and mountain ranges become a plain" (40:4).

Why does Mark begin by the announcement of this gigantic leveling? We have seen that for a magical conception of the world, the social order depends on a respect for differences that are regarded as entirely natural. Consequently, their denial is feared as a threat of chaos. In the mythological realm, which is that of the prologue of Mark, the reminder of the removal of differences indicates that the practice which is to be narrated has brought about a radical upheaval of society. His upheaval is analogous to the mythological end of the world that will definitively reduce the gap between heaven and earth. As Revelation 21.1 puts it: "For the first heaven and the first earth had vanished, and there was no longer any sea." The majority of the mythological stories bring onto the scene two matched heroes who are equal and undifferentiated—usually they are twins like Jacob and Esau in Genesis, or Eteocles and Polyneices in the Oedipus myth. Consequently they are bent on killing each other and prolonging the cycle of violence. In Mark appear in the aorist tense, which is used for narratives, two personages—"John the Baptist appeared" and "Jesus came"—who do not set themselves in opposition but mutually acknowledge each other.[3] Thus the magic circle of violence is broken. It will close in mortally on John and on Jesus, but already the text of Mark testifies to the work of demythologizing, which we shall see carried through to the end.

Before concluding with this prologue, it is necessary to mention again its role as a programmer. We have said that the story has not yet begun, but the text starts to weave in and put into place its codes. It is thus first of all a mythological code, which is already affected by demythologizing. It is also a *topographic* code, that is, a code that refers to the different places where the narrative will unfold.

Here is indicated very clearly an itinerary in four stages: "Jesus came from Nazareth in Galilee"; "he was immersed by John in the Jordan [in Judea]"; he was *tempted* in the wilderness"; and "he returned to Galilee." But the itinerary of Jesus, we shall see, will take place first in Galilee, and then in Jerusalem, which is in Judea. There will be the temptation in Gethsemane and death, and finally the assertion "He will go before you into Galilee . . . as he told you" (16:7).

THE NEXT-TO-THE-LAST AND THE LAST NARRATIVES

A word must still be said about Mark 1:14–15: "Jesus came into Galilee proclaiming the Gospel of God: 'The time has come, the kingdom of God is upon you; repent, and believe the Gospel.' " We are still in the discourse. After the voice of John the Baptist and the voice from heaven, we hear the voice of Jesus. And what it proclaims is "the time has come," that is to say, the end of history announced, we have seen, by the apocalyptic-eschatological texts. Therefore, before its beginning, the narration of the practice of Jesus is referred to as being the *next-to-the-last* narrative. Immediately afterward, "heaven and earth will pass away" (13:31); this means that the mythological difference will be erased and that the sacred primordial time will return. "They will see the Son of Man coming in the clouds with great power and glory" (13:26), and then will come to pass the eschatological "kingdom of God," which is the last story.

We know that the first Christian generation lived in the expectation of the Parousia or return of Jesus. The destruction of Jerusalem and the Temple, the symbolic center of the mythological axis between heaven and earth, marked for them the imminence of the end of the age. That is why we claim to see the effects on Mark of the catastrophe of A.D. 70. But the Parousia was delayed, and the other Gospels that were written a generation later show the effects of this development. They separate the end of the world from the end of Jerusalem.

Chapter 10

A Subversive Narrative

Why should we read the Gospel of Mark today? Everyone has an answer. For my part I say because this text has an effect on me—more of an effect, I admit, than any other text in the world.

It is true that for many years I read it very naively, as I had been taught. I read "Jesus did this, Jesus said that . . ." and I received this message without difficulty. I took the text literally, not being interested in the text itself, any more than in the glass of a window through which I was looking at the landscape. In the same way, at the movies I believed for a long time that the only interesting thing was the story being told. And then I discovered the importance of the framework, the outline, the sequences, the editing, the relation between dialogue and music or noises, and so on. My "readings" of a film multiplied. Not only did I receive more pleasure but I understood better how this pleasure was produced.

It is a little like that for the Bible, as we have begun to notice from one chapter to another. In considering these texts no longer primarily as a transparent glass but as the product of work, we arrived at the means of understanding the secret of the effect the Bible makes on us.

What effect does the text of Mark make on us, and by what means does it achieve this?

A TEARING

Three analogous indications attract our attention:
1. In a series of five sequences about the controversies of Jesus

with the Pharisees in chapters 2 and 3, Mark puts this sentence in the mouth of Jesus: "No one sews a patch of unshrunk cloth on to an old coat; if he does, the patch tears away from it, the new from the old, and leaves a bigger hole" (2:21).

2. At the moment Jesus comes to affirm before the Sanhedrin that he is the Messiah, "the High Priest *tore* his robes" (14:63).

3. Right after the death of Jesus, "the curtain of the temple was torn in two from top to bottom" (15:38).

These three tearings appear very symptomatic of textual work. What the narration of the practice of Jesus does, in effect, is a *tearing* or *schism*, to use the Greek term. The old coat, the robes of the High Priest, the curtain of the Temple—what do they connote? To what code do they refer us? What do they signify if not the official text (tissue) of the Jewish social formation, the "symbolic code" that organizes social relationships, that is to say, essentially the system of purity?

What does the Gospel of Mark do, and what textual work does it perform? It narrates precisely the tearing, the *subversion* of this tissue by the practice of Jesus. In fact, what does it say about this practice?

Protest against the System of Purity

Mark presents Jesus' practice as being the deed of a man of Galilee. Galilee was less "pure" as a country than Judah; its true name was Gelil ha Goyim, which means "the district of the pagans." Jesus' practice is the deed of a common craftsman or carpenter (6:3), who is surrounded by workers of the dominated classes, such as fishermen (1:16–20) and impure people such as publicans and sinners (2:13–15).

What does this practice consist of that its reknown—that is, the narrative spread by public rumor—has reached into all Galilee (1:28) and then to Judah, Jerusalem, Idumea, Transjordan, Tyre, and Sidon (3:8)? The first sequences of the narration tell especially about the healings, which a summary narrative resumes in 1:32–34. "A man possessed of an unclean spirit"—that is, a madman—is brought back to his senses and reintegrated into the social circuit from which his impurity had excluded him (1:23–27). "The mother-in-law of Simon, in bed with a fever" is put back on her feet (1:29–31). A leper—an excluded person who rendered unclean whoever came near—is "cleansed" (1:40–42). A paralytic has his sins forgiven and is invited to arise and walk, which he does (2:1–12). Jesus takes a seat at the table of a publican who as a tax collector for the Romans was impure, and Jesus eats "with publicans and sinners" (2:15 ff.). The companions of Jesus plucked grain on the Sabbath "because they were hungry" (2:23–27). "A man with a withered hand" sees it "restored to health" on a Sabbath day (3:1–5).

After these sequences Mark says: "But the Pharisees . . . began plotting against him with the partisans of Herod to see who they could make away with him" (3:5).

If the practice of Jesus and his group of disciples had this effect on the Pharisees, whose rigorous attachment to the system of purity we have seen, and on the Herodians, who were doubtless the partisans of Herod Antipas, the tetrarch, who was the prince of Galilee and Perea from 4 B.C. to A.D. 39, it is because they felt its subversiveness, which they interpreted as a threat to their situation.

More precisely, if Mark, at the time of his narrating, could show the Pharisees and Herodians reacting in that way, it is because he had set in place earlier the conditions that had to produce that effect. So the practices of Jesus and his disciples must be read as a tearing of the symbolic Jewish tissue. How is that? They all have this in common. They are presented as a rejection of a magical attitude before the fearful violence of death present in madness, fever, leprosy, and paralysis. The system of purity had the purpose specifically of conjuring this violence through the magic of Temple sacrifices and a scrupulous observation of the Law and Sabbath. But this system, which was put into place and run by the ruling classes, had as its primary objective, as we have seen, the maintenance of their power.

In short, the text stamps the practice of Jesus and his people with a reference connotation to the system of the gift that aimed at abolishing injustices in order to establish a fraternal society.

Promoting the System of the Gift

Another group of sequences will permit us to specify the subversiveness of Jesus' practice. Between Mark 6:14 and 8:30 scenes unfold that often center on bread and meals. In addition, they all are situated at the northern frontier of Galilee, or even outside Palestine.

Let us look particularly at the two scenes traditionally called "the feeding of the multitude" (6:30–44; 8:1–10). They function according to the same textual schema of Jesus and his disciples and a hungry crowd; the disciples suggest sending the people "to *buy* themselves something to eat" (6:36) and speak of "two hundred denarii" (6:37); Jesus replies: "How many loaves have you?" (6:38), "*Give* them something to eat" (6:37). The bread is distributed; the crowd is filled. The movement indicated by the text is clear: it is the opposition of *buying* with money to *giving* what they have. What the text exalts is not the multiplying of the loaves but rather the negation of the merchant system that governs exchanges by money and the promotion of the system of the gift in which everything belongs to everyone. In a social organization dominated by those who have in their hands the economic, political, and ideological apparatus, we can have bread only for money. To affirm that we must share the wealth is obviously to introduce a subversion of the system of classes. It is surprising that the rich find that message not saddening" (10:17–22).

Subversion of the Jewish Symbolic Order

A third group of sequences shows how the tearing steadily increases in Mark 10 through 12. Geographically the scene has changed. The band of Jesus and his disciples is en route toward Jerusalem where he will arrive in time for the festivities of the Passover.

Here, the old tissue that is tearing apart is represented by incidents concerned with marriage and divorce (10:1–12); wealth (10:17–27); political power (10:41–45); the Temple as the symbol of Israel (11:12–25 and 12:1–12); Roman taxation (12:13–17); the Law (12:28–34); the scribes (12:38–40); the Temple treasury (12:41–44). It is to be noted that all these points make up a system. They constitute the essential element of the economic, political, and ideological organization of first-century Palestine, as we analyzed it in Chapter 6. Now Mark tells very precisely about its subversion by the practice and word of Jesus. We shall illustrate this by two episodes.

First of all let us consider the sequence of the sterile figtree, the vendors chased from the Temple, and the parable of murderous tenants of the vineyard (11:12-25 and 12:1-12). All these scenes are the same, and they must be read together.

The figtree and the vineyard, in fact, are symbolic images of Israel whose center is the Temple.[1] The figtree is sterile; the vineyard has been taken over by the tenants who no longer recognize the owner (Yahweh, the God of Israel) or his envoys (the prophets); and the Temple has been turned from its role as a house of prayer into a means for commercial benefit. Thus through the simple textual proximity of these three scenes, Mark has us read the effect of the presence of Jesus at Jerusalem. This presence showed the perversion which the society of classes had brought about in the area of Palestine, and in so doing it subverted it. This is certainly the way "the chief priests, lawyers, and elders" (11:27) interpreted it: "then they began to look for a way to arrest him, for they saw that the parable [of the tenants of the vineyard] was aimed at them" (12:12).

It is no less clear in the scene of the taxes for Caesar (12:13-17).[2] The textual analysis is even more interesting here since the envoys of the high priests who pose the question "Are we or are we not permitted to pay taxes to the Roman emperor?" are not interested in the reply. They have set up the question as a trap and, whatever his answer, Jesus must be taken in it. In fact, if he replies, "no, we must not pay," they will accuse him before the Romans, which is what Luke actually reports (23:2). If Jesus answers "we must pay," the crowd that admires him as a Zealot Messiah (see chapter 11 below) will abandon him to the hatred of the chief priests. Now the text shows here once again the movement and the subversion introduced by Jesus. Confronted with the coin symbolizing both the Roman occupation and the power of the ruling classes collaborating with the Romans—that is what "belonging to Caesar" means—Jesus given an answer that shows that his adversaries are simply forgetting what "belongs to God." And what belongs to God if not Israel—a figtree made sterile by its exploiters, a vineyard stolen by the tenants from its owner, the Temple, which is a symbol of the society of classes? Thus the instruction "Pay Caesar what is due to Caesar and pay God what is due to God" means reconquering from Caesar, that is, the Jewish sub-Asiatic system integrated into Roman imperialism, what belongs to God. The tearing apart is at its height.

The Body of Jesus, the Poor, and the Shared Bread

The tearing apart will reach completion when Mark shows how the new tissue takes the place of the old. This is the object of the sequence in 14:1–24. While "the chief priests and the doctors of the law were trying to devise some cunning plan to seize him and put him to death" (14:1), and while Judas the sicarius was preparing to give them the means by revealing where Jesus was hiding (14:10–11, 43–47), the text proposes three scenes that are linked structurally: the anointing at Bethany; preparations for the Passover supper; and the institution of the Eucharist.

First, we must read 14:12–16. This scene resembles surprisingly 11:1–11 on the messianic entry into Jerusalem. Let's put them side by side:

11:1 [Jesus] sent two of his disciples with these instructions: "Go to the village opposite . . . you will find . . . say, ' Our Master needs it. . . . ' " So they went off, and found. . . .	14:13 [Jesus] sent two of his disciples with these instructions: "Go into the city . . . you will meet . . . say: 'The Master says. . . .' " Then the disciples went off . . . and they found. . . .

This parallel construction indicates a relationship. On the one hand, Jesus is going to enter Jerusalem and expose the perversion of the figtree, vineyard, and Temple sequence. On the other hand, Jesus is going to enter an anonymous house to represent the replacement of the Temple by something else.

This something else is already designated by the anointing at Bethany. Here the *body* of Jesus is anointed with perfume (a messianic connotation). His sentence "The poor you will always have with you . . . ; me you will not always have with you"—the Greek text puts the verbs in the present tense—signals a textual opposition: the presence of the poor with the disciples, and the absence of Jesus from his disciples.

And that is where we must see the Eucharist. This scene, which picks up again the schema of the multiplying of the loaves, presents both the body of Jesus, which now assumes at the center of the new space created by his ministry the role the Temple played at the center of the Jewish space, and the announced absence of this body, which is shown symbolically by the sharing of bread and doing good for the poor. When the narrative of Mark first circulated, the disciples of Jesus were meeting together in fact "to share the common life, to break bread" as well as "to hear the apostles teach" (Acts 2:42). This means that Jesus was henceforth present among them in the sharing of the bread with the poor and in the telling of his practice.

THE SUBVERSION

And the telling continues in their midst to promote the tearing or subversion. We can now synthesize its effects.

On the Economic Level

Exchange value defines the aptitude of an object for being exchanged for other objects and transforms all products of human work as well as the workers themselves into saleable commodities. To replace "buy bread with money" with "give what you have" is to subvert the fetishism of merchandise that transforms social relationships into the buying and selling of things. (Marx also calls this process "reification" or thingifying.) It is at the same time the restoration of the use value , the utility belonging to each thing, and the sharing of this use with everyone.

But we must note immediately that for different reasons this revolution was impossible in the Jewish sub-Asiatic system and in the Roman imperial system. In the former, in fact, the small peasant landowners were completely dominated politically by the caste in power. In the latter, slavery blocked the advance of the productive forces and therefore prohibited a reversal of the relationships of production.

Limited politically and economically in this way, the subversion brought about by the narration of the ministry of Jesus was therefore, as we shall see later, rapidly retrieved by the dominant classes, but it has never ceased to cause a tearing which doubtless can be called utopian and which has made a great impact on the course of history.

On the Political Level

The narration of Mark constantly undermines the system of roles in the social organization by reintegrating those who have been excluded—the insane, the sick, the unclean, and the poor— and by threatening the forces in power. In addition, as we shall see in the next chapter, the text often has Jesus crossing the borders of Israel and ends with a rendezvous in Galilee, which thereby geographically subverts the symbolic field centered on Jerusalem. But the most important point probably lies elsewhere.

It is first of all in the constant affirmation that power and life are not on the side of those who hold the upper hand—the rich, the masters, and the chiefs—but rather on the side of the little people, children, and servants. It is the intuition that Friedrich Nietzsche rediscovered: the force of arms reveals the profound weakness of those who depend on it to stay in power.

There is more. The subversive dynamism of this narration comes, as René Girard has shown, from the fact that it *forces violence to show its hand*—that violence of death which the magic of the system of purity sought to summon.[3] By imprinting itself upon this violence, the subversion forces violence to exteriorize itself and to become objective. In denouncing violence, in renouncing and exposing it, Jesus is shown as the one who puts an end to the sacrificial system and creates a space for the reconciled life where reciprocity is possible.[4]

On the Ideological Level

Finally, it is more than clear that Mark builds his narrative in such a way that he tears bit by bit at the Jewish ideological tissue. But the question raised then is: What did the Christians of Rome in A.D 71 have to do with that tissue? To understand this question, we must fall back on a sequence of which we have not yet spoken: chapter 13, the "eschatological discourse." The scenario is set on the Mount of Olives, opposite the Temple, of which Jesus has just declared, "Not one stone will be left upon another; all will be thrown down" (13:2). And his first four disciples, Peter, James, John, and Andrew, ask him: "Tell us when will this happen? What will be the sign when the fulfillment of all this is at hand?" There follows a long discourse of Jesus that is entirely in the future tense and very explicitly addressed, although in the coded language of apocalypses, to the readers of Mark more than to the four disciples. Mark writes, "Let the reader understand" (13:14). Wars, rumors of wars, and famines probably refer to the Jewish War of 66-70. Betrayals ("You will be handed over . . ." [13:9]): torture, trials, and death penalties refer doubtless to the recent persecution of Nero (64-67). The statement "but before the end the Gospel must be proclaimed to all nations" (13-10) indicates the birth of Christian communities throughout the empire (see the letters of Paul). "The abomination of desolation" (13:14), which is sometimes translated as "the odious devastator," certainly designates the fall of Jerusalem and the profanation and burning of the Temple by the Romans in A.D. 70. The rest—the flight to the mountains, and so on—describes, in fact, the reign of terror throughout a Judea devastated by the legions.

But suddenly, beginning with 13:24, the discourse takes another turn. "After that distress [thus after A.D. 70], the sun will be darkened . . . , the stars will come falling from the sky . . . , they then will see the Son of Man coming in the clouds with great power and glory . . . and he will . . . gather his chosen from . . . the farthest bounds of earth to the farthest bounds of heaven." This involves, obviously, the mythological code. Here is the true conclusion of the text of Mark. Taking up the threads of the code that served to weave the prologue, it closes on the effacement of the heaven/earth/abyss differences which permitted the narration in the time of history.

Henceforth, Mark says to the Christians of Rome, the time is fulfilled, and the Parousia is near: "The present generation will live to see it all" (13.30). We have noted already, and we shall take up this point again, that the Son of Man did not return in the time of that generation, and that the other Gospels testify to the progressive extinction of an eschatological expectation of the imminent end of the world.

It remains for us to verify our hypothesis. Mark is addressing the Christians of Rome shortly after A.D. 70. By putting into the lips of Jesus the announcement of the end of Jerusalem (and of all the Jewish system whose tissue he has undermined) and at the same time the promise of his return very soon, Mark added to the veracity of the second promise by the recent fulfillment of the first one. In so doing, he aimed at keeping his readers alert, vigilant (see 13:33), and "awake" (13:37).

Chapter 11

Topology and Strategy

If we try to trace the travels indicated by the text on a map of Palestine, we are in for a lot of trouble. This shows once again that Mark's Gospel is not a life of Jesus to be followed word for word, with respect to what is "signified." It is rather a literary narration that tries in its own way to restore the dynamics of the ministry of Jesus. Somewhat in the same way a picture does not represent its subject, but seeks to suggest its impression through forms and colors.

This is why we shall not make a topographically detailed description of places, but a *topology*, that is, a study of the qualitative properties and relative positions of geometric beings, regardless of their shape and size. So we shall not follow the itineraries of Jesus, but we shall detect the shapes that structure this or that part of the narrative.

It is true that the most obvious figures are first of all *geographic*: we have seen that the prologue of Mark programs the four great settings where the story will take place: Galilee; Judea; the sites for the temptation and death; and Galilee again. But these spaces are above all symbolic. Since the codes of the text are Jewish, everything is centered or magnetized, in a way by Judea, Jerusalem, and the Temple. The practice of Jesus begins outside this magnetic pole; it is off center. When it approaches the center, the compass needle jumps around, the codes clash, the old tissue is torn, and there is confrontation. But after the death of Jesus, the narration takes off again toward Galilee. "He [Jesus] is going on before you" (16:7), that is, toward the pagans. This is the general structure that commands the dynamics of the text. But we must look into it more closely.

THE CIRCLES

Throughout this narration, concentric circles frequently occur around the person of Jesus: "He was soon spoken of *all over the district*" (1:28); "the whole town was there *gathered at the door*" (1:33); "people kept coming to him *from all quarters*" (1:45); "such a crowd collected that the *space in front of the door* was not big enough to hold them" (2:2); "so they opened up the roof *over the place* where Jesus was" (2:4); "many bad characters—tax gatherers and others—were *seated* with him and his disciples" (2:15); "some doctors of the law who were Pharisees noticed him *eating*, . . . and said to his disciples" (2:16); in a synagogue Jesus said to the man: "Come and *stand out here*" (3:3); on the mountain, Jesus "called the men *he wanted*; . . . he appointed *twelve*" (3:13); at the house "the crowd *collected* around them" (3:20); "a crowd was *sitting around* outside" (3:32); "and looking around at those who were sitting *in the circle* about him" (3:34); "when he was *alone*, the Twelve and others who were *round him* questioned him . . ." (4:10).

The scene of the woman with the issue of blood (5:21–43) is particularly clear. The woman must cross through the crowd and the disciples in order to touch Jesus; "the apostles [the Twelve] now *rejoined* Jesus" (6:30); "all who *touched* him were cured" (6:56); "the Pharisees with some doctors of the law who had come from Jerusalem *met him*" (7:1); "when he *had left* the people and gone indoors his disciples questioned him" (7:17); "then he called the people to him, as well as his *disciples*" (8:34); "Jesus took Peter, James, and John with him and led them up a high mountain where *they were alone*" (9:2); "when they came back to the disciples they saw a large crowd *surrounding* them and lawyers arguing with them" (9:14); "he sat down, called the Twelve, . . . took a child, set him *in front of them*" (9:35–36); "[in Judea] a crowd *gathered around him* once again" (10:1); "he took *the Twelve aside*" (10:32); "[in the Temple] the chief priests, lawyers, and elders came *to him*" (11:27); "they were afraid of the *peo-*

ple" (12:12); "a number of Pharisees and men of Herod's party *were sent* to trap him" (12:13); "next Sadducees came *to him"* (12:18); "one of the lawyers . . . *came forward"* (12:28); "standing opposite the Temple treasury . . . he called his *disciples* to him" (12:41–43); "sitting on the Mount of Olives he was questioned by *Peter, James, John, and Andrew"* (13:3); "as they [the Twelve] *sat at supper"* (14:18); "[at] Gethsemane, he said to his *disciples"* (14:32); "he took *Peter* and *James* and *John* with him" (14:33); "Judas, *one of the Twelve,* appeared, and with him a crowd armed with swords and cudgels, sent by the chief priests, lawyers, and elders. . . . [Judas] *stepped forward.* . . . Then they *seized him* and held him fast" (14:43–46); "then they *led* Jesus away to the High Priest's courtyard, where the chief priests, elders, and doctors of the law were all assembling" (14:53); "then they *led* him away and handed him over to Pilate" (15:1); "the soldiers *took him inside* . . . and called together the whole company" (15:16); "two bandits [read "terrorists"] were crucified with him, one on his *right* and the other on his *left"* (15:27); "the centurion who was standing *opposite* him" (15:39); "a number of women were also present, *watching* from a distance" (15:40).

This long list of quotations enables us to discern how the text situates people around the person of Jesus. Closest are Peter, James, John, and sometimes Andrew; then the Twelve; then the disciples; farther out the crowd; still farther out the scribes (lawyers and doctors of the law), the Pharisees, Sadducees, chief priests, and elders around whom circles spread that are opposed to the first ones.

In the opening sequences, the crowd is drawn by the fame of Jesus—the narrative of his practice. This displeases the people in power; the Pharisees and Herodians begin to plot against him (3:6). But already Jesus is not going to let himself be hemmed in by the crowd: "Let us move on" (1:38). He tries to stop the narrative of his ministry: "Be sure you say nothing to anybody" (1:44). He also tries to escape from those who turn out to be his adversaries, "but [Jesus] stayed outside in the open country" (1:45).

However, as if in spite of himself, his person continues to create a sort of "magnetic field." The text very strongly gives the impression that the figure of Jesus works like a magnetic force, a pole of attraction. The crowds are irresistibly drawn to him; pros-

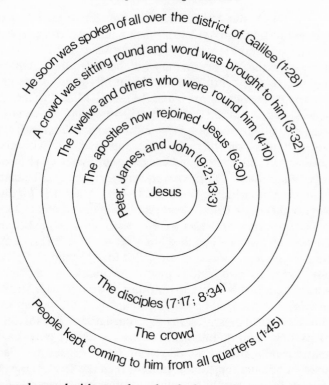

A crowd armed with swords and cudgels, sent by the chief priests, lawyers, and elders (14:43)

A number of Pharisees and men of Herod's party were sent to trap him (12:13)

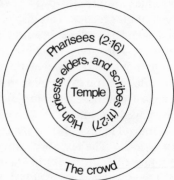

trate bodies are set again on their feet. It suffices only to be in contact with this source of energy to receive a kind of discharge.

And that is exactly why the representatives and owners of the other magnetic field—the Jewish system centered on the Temple—feel the appearance of this one as a threat. The practice of Jesus creates a counterforce. The concentric waves that spread out from Jesus and that draw the crowds to him also reach the center of a series of opposing waves that become more and more violent. There is thus a clash between them, a conflict of forces.

The antagonism reaches its height when the field of Jesus approaches geographically the Jewish field, that is, when Jesus arrives at Jerusalem and enters the Temple. Faced with the threatening waves of the adverse field, Jesus is protected by the circle the crowd draws around him. But this crowd is also a circle of the Jewish field and dependent, especially economically, on the Temple. (We have seen that the majority of the inhabitants of Jerusalem lived off the Temple.) Consequently the strategy of Jesus' adversaries will be to take him when he is cut off from the crowd. Knowing this, Jesus hides. Every night he leaves Jerusalem and takes refuge in a safe place (11:11-19; 14:3).

The decisive confrontation occurs under unfavorable conditions for Jesus. Thanks to his betrayal by someone near to him, his enemies find him away from the crowd. Heavily armed, they "lay hands upon him and *arrested* him." These words are characteristic: the center of the Jesus field has just been arrested, as when one turns off a motor. From that moment in the text Jesus will be like a direct object of the verbs "to take," "to take away," "to lead away."[1] He will be like an arrested source of energy that requires towing . . . until the public discharge on the bare mountain of Golgotha, the "place of the skull."

THE BOAT

From Mark 3:9, however, another figure appears—the boat that permits Jesus not to be crowded by the people on the shore of Lake Tiberius. This must also be read at the level of strategy. Jesus does not want to be locked in by the crowd. He can tell that the crowd does not have exactly the same projects as he. He gives himself some space (4:1). And as if he feared that his disciples might be influenced by the crowd, he takes them with him in the boat, back and forth from shore to shore along the lake (4:35; 5:1–21; 6:32, 45, 53; 8:10, 14). The beginning and the end of this sequence of coming and going are very clearly marked. They begin at 3:7 when the crowds arrive in concentric waves from all the points of the horizon: Judea, Transjordan, and Phoenicia. The end comes in 8:29 when Peter says to Jesus, "You are the Messiah."

What is therefore the point of this sequence? What effect is it intended to produce? One sign attracts our attention. Mark insists a great deal on the incomprehension of the disciples: "He said to them: 'You do not understand?' " (4:13); "so far as they were *able* to receive it" (4:33); "Have you *no* faith even now?" (4:40); "for they had not *understood* . . ." (6:52); "Are you as *dull* as the rest?" (7:18); "Have you *no inkling* yet?" (8:17); "Do you still not *understand?*" (8:21). And just before Peter "understands," a symbolic episode represents this progressive enlightenment of the minds of the disciples: the healing in two stages of the blind man of Bethsaida (8:22–26). First, the man only half sees, as in a fog: "I see men; they look like trees, but they are walking about." It is only in a second stage that he sees "everything clearly." Does not this little scene fit perfectly what is happening in the minds of the disciples? All during these boat crossings, they discover little by little the main thread of Jesus' practice, which they observe and share in. This practice makes sense only in the light that Peter brings: the power that creates this counterfield is messianic. But we have been able to discover the means by which the text produces this recognition.

THE ROAD

Hardly had Mark put on the lips of Peter his expression of insight into the practice of Jesus than the narrative changed direction abruptly. First of all, it changed geographically: from Caesarea Philippi in Trachonitis in the far north (8:27) it crossed Galilee (9:30) to Capernaum on the shores of the lake (9:33) and then headed for Judea (10:1).

And from that time a new image appeared—the *road:* "they . . . made a *journey*" (9:30); "What were you arguing about on the *way?"* (9:33); ". . . on the *way* they had been discussing . . ." (9:34); "as he was starting out on a *journey* . . ." (10:17); "they were on the *road"* (10:32); "a blind beggar was seated at the *roadside"* (10:46); ". . . and followed him on the *road"* (10:52).

Now this road began at Caesarea Philippi and stopped at Jerusalem (chapter 11). Consequently, Mark gave it the function of representing a strategy—a road goes somewhere; it is a project in motion—worked out by the Jesus field to meet the adverse field on its own ground—Jerusalem, the Temple.

But looking more closely, we also perceive that this road, where the disciples walked behind Jesus (10:32), was the place where a confrontation occurred. Everything happened, in fact, as if Peter's declaration had not clarified entirely the meaning of Jesus' practice for his disciples. They did not seem to see things as he did; their strategies differed. For example, "Peter began to *rebuke* him" (8:32); "Jesus *rebuked* Peter" (8:33); "the disciples *rebuked* them [those who brought the children to Jesus], but when Jesus saw this he was *indignant"* (10:13); "the disciples were *amazed"* (10:24); "they were more *astonished* than ever" (10:26); "the disciples were filled with *awe,* . . . afraid" (10:32). All these verbs are extremely vigorous and show the contrast or opposition between Jesus and his disciples. Obviously his strategy was not theirs; the closer they got to Jerusalem, the less they seemed to agree on what they ought to do there. And the messianic entry into Jerusalem probably marked the climax of this misunderstanding because shortly afterward, at the decisive moment of the encounter, all the disciples abandoned Jesus and ran away (14:50).

THE ZEALOT STRATEGY

What is this divergence? It lies in the fact that the disciples' strategy, which is also that of the crowd, was very likely a Zealot strategy.

It will be remembered that the Zealots were essentially peasants who had left the great landholdings where they were overexploited and who lived by pillage and robbery. Ideologically close to the Pharisees, they despised and hated the chief priests whose legitimacy they challenged and whose collaboration with the pagan Roman occupation forces they condemned. Their strategic aim was to chase the Romans out by guerrilla and terrorist tactics and to reestablish the Jewish social organization (thus the sub-Asian system) in all its purity. They therefore could be called reactionaries. For them, the awaited Messiah was to be a leader of the people—anti-Roman and anti-high priests—who would restore the kingdom of David.

The Palestinian crowds, which were made up principally of peasants and the poor, were very much influenced by Zealot ideas. And among the disciples, as we have seen, there probably were two or three Zealot partisans: Simon the Zealot and Judas Iscariot (from *sicarius,* or "dagger"). Perhaps we should include Simon-Peter Barjona (from "terrorist"). It is not surprising, therefore, that the strategy of the disciples reflected this viewpoint. It is undoubtedly what the episodes mean that marked the road toward Jerusalem: "they had been discussing who was the greatest" (9:34); at which Jesus presents a little child (9:36); the fascination with riches (10:23–27); the implicit question of Peter: "We here have left everything to become your followers" (10:28), by which he was asking: "What will be our recompense?"; the request of the sons of Zebedee in 10:25–40 to have the chief seats next to the conquering Messiah.

THE STRATEGY OF JESUS

Over against this strategy, Mark never failed to delineate that of Jesus: the strategy of a child, of a poor man, a servant and slave. The Messiah presented by Jesus did not have the flair of the dominating conqueror. And the entry into Jerusalem, as a kind of popular triumph, was described by Mark with all the necessary references to indicate the specific character of this Messiah. The young ass recalled the prophecy of Zechariah 9:9: "Rejoice, rejoice, daughter of Zion, shout aloud, daughter of Jerusalem for see, your king is coming to you, his cause won, his victory gained, humble and mounted on an ass, on a foal, the young of a she-ass. He shall banish chariots from Ephraim and war-horses from Jerusalem." As for the robes spread before him on the ground, they evoked the scene of 2 Kings 9:13 where, at the call of the prophet Elisha, Jehu rebelled against King Joram and Queen

Mother Jezebel: "They snatched up their cloaks and spread them under him on the stones of the steps, and sounded the trumpet and shouted, 'Jehu is king.' '' In short, these connotations were clear: the Messiah presented by Jesus was prophetic and anti-royal; he belonged to the system of the gift as opposed to that of purity. The scenes that followed in the Temple showed him denouncing the sterility of the Temple system at the same time that he rejected the Zealot strategy of refusing to pay the tax.

It is therefore evident that Mark did not want to present Jesus as a Zealot Messiah. But that does not mean, as the traditional idealist exegesis claims, that Mark made him a spiritual Messiah, abandoning the temporal domain to the jurisdiction of Caesar.

Our materialist reading enables us to see here a *strategy* that might be called *"communist, nonrevolutionary,* and *internationalist."* It was communist because, as we saw in the preceding chapter, it aimed at reestablishing sharing, the value of use as against the value of exchange. It was nonrevolutionary because the economic and political conditions of the Jewish sub-Asian system integrated into a slave-holding Roman imperial system did not permit a revolutionary transformation of the relationships of production. It was internationalist because the narrative constantly crossed the borders of Palestine and ended by bursting out toward Galilee in the direction of the pagan countries.

Let us bring together now all the images of our topology. The power and energy that surged from the person (in a geometric or structural sense) of Jesus spread around him concentric circles that tended to enclose him in the image of a Zealot Messiah, which he rejected. Having created a prophetic-messianic counterfield antagonistic to the Jewish field, he set out on the *road* to confront that field on its own ground, the Temple. He was betrayed, abandoned, arrested, and executed, but the *circle* of the messianic *counterfield* continued its *road* toward the whole world.[2]

Chapter 12

Class Readings of the Scriptures

As we continue our reading at various points and look for the codes that weave Mark's Gospel together, we will now take up the *analytical code*. This gathers all the analyses, readings, and interpretations of the narration of Jesus' practice that different personages made within the text itself. We have already noticed that the crowds and the disciples made a Zealot reading of it, and that the scribes, chief priests, and elders interpreted it as a threat to their power.

But the personage of Jesus made his strategic decisions himself, as we have just seen, in relation to the analysis he made of the readings and strategies of the other protagonists.

A HALL OF MIRRORS

Let us make a comparison. During a card game we try to discover what cards our partner and opponents hold. We try to find out their strategy and consequently develop our own. So life is like a game crisscrossed with observances of the rules. Everyone knows only a part of the totality of the game, and it is the continuous reading of the mutual observances that allows this or that choice. Indeed, perhaps that explains the reason we like to read stories for they tell about observances whose interpretation helps us decipher what we are experiencing ourselves. Or they may help us hide our experience or beautify it. Cervantes, Stendhal, and Dostoevski serve as reading grids for our own observances, as on another level do such popular pastimes as comic books and soap operas.

At any rate, this is the way Mark's Gospel functions. A prime example is 2:23-27. The disciples passed through the harvest fields and plucked grain and ate it. The Pharisees took note of this practice and made of it the following *reading:* the Law forbids these actions on the Sabbath day; the disciples are therefore struck with uncleanness unto death by the Law. Jesus opposed this with *another reading* of this practice, but he did it in a curious manner. He told the story of another practice, that of David and his companions (1 Sam. 21:2-7). Now if the two narratives are set in parallel, we find the following:

1. Why do your disciples	1. David and his men,
2.	2. when they were in need and were hungry,
3. pluck grain	3. ate the sacred bread
4. on the Sabbath day,	4. in the house of God,
5. which is not allowed?	5. which is not allowed except for priests.

What leaps out is that phrase 2 has no parallel in the first column. This is precisely what Jesus left for the Pharisees to read. If the disciples did this, it is because they were hungry. The Pharisees were unable to read that message, enclosed as they were in their legalistic system of the clean and the unclean. Their analysis of the practice of Jesus and his disciples was determined by their function in the class structure. And what Jesus showed them was that they ended up by not being able to read even the official text of their own ideology. In transforming into the Law or a system of prohibitions the founding narratives, they perverted the role of those stories.

The following scene was also characteristic (3:1-6). Here the mechanism of reading and analysis was put in place before the practice occurred. In effect, Jesus knew then that the Pharisees "were watching him to see whether he would cure him [the man with the withered arm] on the Sabbath, so that they could bring a charge against him." So Jesus asked the sick man or outcast to stand up before everybody, so that his need and handicap might be evident. And he gave the key to the reading of what he was going to do. For him the opposition was not between respecting the Sabbath and not respecting the Sabbath but between doing good and doing evil, between saving life and killing. Once again it was the system of the gift vis-à-vis the system of purity.

Thus the narration of the practice of Jesus, reflected as in a hall of mirrors by the readings of different personages, constantly shed light on their strategies. It functioned as a grid of interpretation for the various ministries. All readers of Mark were thus led to situate themselves in relation to this narrative and consequently to read by this grid their own practice.

THE ANALYTICAL CODE: ALL PERSONS READ
IN RELATION TO THEIR OWN SITUATION

One very special sequence is going to offer us, so to speak, the *way to use* the analytical code in Mark. It is the famous parable of the sower (4:1-9, 13-20). This fictitious narrative related by Jesus to the whole crowd from the boat (4:1-9) was, in fact, decoded for the disciples (4:13-20). It unfolded in three steps—the seed, the growth, and the harvest—and in four different places. The seed was the same in the four soils, but the growth was not the same. It was therefore the soils that determined the work of growing. Now the decoding indicates that the soils represented the readers of the word (that is to say, as we have seen, the narration of the practice of Jesus). Therefore, this parable gives, in a way, the theory of the reading of this narrative. In relation to their places, that is, the places they have in the social structure, the different actors read, decided, and acted. Thus the scribes, chief priests, elders, and their associates analyzed according to their class position. The crowd of peasants and artisans whose situation was ambiguous was divided. The disciples were those who had taken a step on the road outside the circles of the ruling system. Everyone was called to do the same. The narration of the practice of Jesus was to be received by all those who wanted to break with the oppressive power, be converted, and follow Jesus. This is why, in fact, Mark never showed Jesus preaching or teaching. He acted and proposed the grids for the reading of his ministry. All persons can open their eyes and ears (Mark often spoke of seeing and hearing when he used the analytical code). But Jesus never explained what he did or what he wanted. He left his hearers and readers free to decide for themselves.

QUESTIONS AND ANSWERS— SIGNIFIER AND SIGNIFIED

This is why Jesus never answered the questions of those whose situation showed them to be adversaries. In fact, as we have seen in relation to the taxes of Caesar, their questions were never true interrogations but a mechanism designed to trap him. A good example was the discussion in 11:27–33, which is located between the episode of the withered fig-tree or Temple and the parable of the murderous keepers of the vineyard. Here, "the chief priests, lawyers, and elders came to him and said: 'By what authority are you acting like this? Who gave you authority to act in this way?' " An idealist reader of Mark would be surprised here that Jesus did not answer simply: "I do that because I am the Son of God!" But Mark did not function that way; he took care to repeat the word "authority" twice (*exousia*=power, which is what these personages, in fact, possessed). It was not coincidental; what really mattered here was clearly the power over the gathered crowd that the chief priests held and Jesus threatened. Their question did not have for them (and consequently for a materialist reader) any interest on the level of the "signified." But the question appears as a textual work of the "signifiers" or the words, and its purpose is to obtain a strategic result: to find some weak point in Jesus in order to "arrest him" (12:12) and to stop his subversive practice. Facing this strategy, Jesus deftly feinted. He was careful not to reply on the level of the "signified"; he set up a little textual mechanism also which was purely strategic: "I will ask you a question. . . . The baptism of John: was it from God, or from men?" And the others never sought for an instant to give him a true or frank answer (terms which would be idealist here). Their only concern was strategic. They carefully weighed the value of exchange of the two answers possible in the eyes of the crowd or "the people" (11:32) that attended this debate and that was the true stake in the game. Finally, they gave no reply, and neither did Jesus. From this point of view, therefore (at the level of the signified), it was a stalemate. But at the strategic level (the textual mechanism of the signifiers), the text made Jesus' adversaries confess at the same time their class status (*exousia* or power) and their murderous project toward Jesus. That is what Jesus showed in the following scene with the killers in the vineyard, which the chief priests interpreted perfectly as being aimed at them (12:12).

We have just seen here once again that only materialist readings can take into account the textual work that weaves the codes of Mark. At first, accustomed to the idealist reading, we have perhaps feared losing the transparency of the text and its apparent simplicity. But the austere work of decoding permits us on second thought to better appreciate its real function.

"HOW, HE DOES NOT KNOW": NARRATION AND CONTINGENCY

Two small parables will give us the opportunity to go further. Coming after the one about the sower (which would be better called "the parable of the soils," as we have seen), they take up again the same image of seeds and growth that are borrowed from agricultural production. It is first of all the story of the "grain which grows of itself" (4:26–29). The chief personage here is the sower (this is the true parable of the sower), and what is said of the work of his practice in sowing is very interesting: "He goes to bed at night and gets up in the morning, and the seed sprouts and grows—how, he does not know."

Inversely to the parable of the soils, Mark's Gospel does not furnish the decoding of this parable. But it does not seem very difficult. We know, in fact, that the sower is Jesus and that what he sows is the narration of his ministry in the eyes and ears of the people. Now what the text says is that the narration germinates and grows among the hearers *without Jesus' knowing how.* Mark poses here, in a way, the narrative principle of all storytelling: the personages only *discover* bit by bit what is happening, the mutual effect of their practices, as the narration advances, just as card-players discover the game as it is played out, with the chance of the tricks but in relation to their readings and strategies. We understand the textual importance of this little parable if we remember that the idealist reading of the Gospel always claims to follow in the story of Jesus the effects of a predestination linked to his status as the Son of God. We shall see how Mark himself witnesses to this concern, but here the contingent character of the narrative must be underlined. What makes a narration is precisely that it relates a practice with its effects, the different readings of these effects, and the strategies that spring from them. In order for Mark's textual logic to be consistent, one cannot know in advance what is going to happen except at another textual level—the mythological—like the demons that "recognize" in Jesus the Messiah. (Or one might know at the theological level, as we shall see later on.)

THE FUTURE OF THE NARRATION

The second little parable is famous; it is the parable of the mustard seed (4:20–32). What is it about? A seed again—that is to say, the narration of the practice of Jesus. It is called "smaller than any seed in the ground at its sowing." Mark therefore sets the narration of the practice of Jesus over against all the narrations of the world, all the practices that are spoken about, and he calls this the smallest one. He characterizes it by what differentiates it from the great narratives, those that tell of the great practices of the great people of this world. But this little seed "springs up and grows taller than any other plant, and forms branches so large that the birds can settle in its shade." What hope fills this text! And how it must have inspired the Christians of Rome in A.D. 71!

But here once again there is an eschatological pointer. "The birds of the air" refers inevitably to the mythological code; it is the end of the world, the coming of the kingdom of God, which Mark announces here. And he underlines the fact that among all the narratives of all practices only that of Jesus will end up in heaven. All the other practices whose true smallness will have been revealed will be excluded. It is needless to recall once again that the ruin of Jerusalem had just given the readers of Mark an apparent confirmation of these words.

Chapter 13

The Narration Poses the Question: Who Is Jesus?

The classic detective story, for example, one by Agatha Christie, poses only one question: "Who dunnit?" And it undertakes to formulate all possible hypotheses, saving the right one for the end. What it proposes to the reader is to exchange a few hours of reading for the pleasure of competing with the author (or the detective who represents the author), although the game is not a fair one since the author tries to throw the reader off the track. But all the pleasure is in that difficulty.

All narrations work this way. Contemporary linguists have shown that all stories, for example, can be grouped in a few simple structures, consisting of posing and solving one or several difficulties: a hiding place to discover, exploits to perform, trials to endure, a personage to identify, a road to find.[1] From the labors of Hercules to Snow White, it is always a matter of proposing to the hearer or reader a textual journey that results in seeking something, a kind of quest (cf. the Holy Grail of the knights of the Round Table) in which *desire* plays hide and seek with itself.

Psychoanalysis permits us to go further here in a materialist approach. In effect, those who undergo analysis are trying to rediscover in a way the lost thread that holds together their existence or body—this text where all the roads we have traveled or that cross through us are inscribed unconsciously. In speaking, through the chance association of words, images, and ideas, persons being psychoanalyzed try to pick up the thread of the discourse that constitutes them, to reknit the codes, to reweave the pattern.

We see how the psychoanalytic method is close to that of linguistics. It is not surprising if linguistics borrows a few of its concepts from psychoanalysis. Thus "desire is the insistence by which the signifying chain is animated, in that the signifier lacks its own completeness."[2] We can translate as follows. A text is a chain, a structure of signifiers animated by the desire for something that is missing, an emptiness around which the text orders itself to mark it, to mask it, or to fill it. From the *Odyssey* to the *Divine Comedy*, from *Pantagruel* to *Moby Dick* and *Ulysses*, is this not the program, in effect, of all the great literary works (not to speak of the other arts)?

So why do we have the Gospel of Mark, which is not a literary masterpiece? Why is it still read? Why has it not lost its interest? To understand the reason, perhaps we must return precisely to its function, the response it activates, the secret desire it evokes.

A MESSAGE OF HAPPINESS

Like all narrations, as we have seen, this Gospel traces its own program from the beginning. Consider its title—"The Good News of Jesus the Messiah." Immediately the enigma is posed. Why is it good news that Jesus is the Messiah? The prologue seems to give the answer. The divinity or heaven has designated this man as the "Son of God." But it is an answer in a mythological code; it only functions on that level. And the narration is not satisfied with that! This is why it constantly brushes off the demons that also "know" who Jesus is. The narration of the practice is what must bring the answer; that is the exchange proposed for our reading.

And little by little, in fact, the practice of Jesus is seen to be messianic: to liberate suffering and outcast bodies, to invite people to a life of sharing rather than the reign of money, to challenge the repressive power of class domination, to disclose the emptiness and sterility of the social system. The practice is indeed seen to rediscover the prophetic vein of Elijah, Elisha, Amos, and Jeremiah. It is seen to reopen the founding narratives in order to implement, by their grid, the reading of present practices. It is seen to inaugurate the messianic era of human relationships, which are finally reciprocal and fraternal.

So it seems normal that at the end of the pedagogical and strategic crisscrossing on the lake Peter could declare: "You are the Messiah." But the ambiguity persisted. The Zealotism of the disciples was manifestly rejected by Jesus. Their own happiness would have been to see him seize power and reign with them over a society of classes in which they would be the new ruling class. This was not the happiness which the practice of Jesus pointed to. Witness his response to the implicit question of Peter: "We have left everything to become your followers." (The implication was: What happiness do you promise us in exchange?) Jesus stated:

> I tell you this: there is no one who has given up home, brothers, or sisters, mother, father or children, or land, for my sake and for the Gospel, who will not receive in this age a hundred times as much—houses, brothers and sisters, mothers and children, and land—and persecutions besides; and in the age to come eternal life. But many who are first will be last and the last first [10:28-31].

There are three periods in this response:

1. You should leave the social system, making a clean break with it. (It has been noted that this is not a matter of leaving one's wife!) You should make this break because of Jesus, that is to say, in the impulse of his liberating ministry, and because of the good news (cf. 1:15 "the time has come"). This means in view of eschatology and the coming kingdom.

2. From this time forward this break will bring about a hundredfold fruition of everything left behind, except for the father, doubtless because there is "only one Father" (cf. Matt. 23:9).

3. In the age to come—the kingdom of God—this break will be worth eternal life.

What does this mean? What happiness is given by the break with the dominant social code? It is the happiness that is the result of the suppression of the relationships of power in a society of classes, where market value destroys the use of things and human reciprocity. The establishment of relationships of nonpower, of nonvalue, or nonfetishism will avoid violence and death better than magic rites. That is happiness here on earth. And the end of the world and of history will prove that this happiness is eternal.

But Mark's Gospel shows at once that the disciples understood none of this, since James and John outdo themselves requesting the best seats in the "glory" which they consider to be at hand.

The disciples' incomprehension reveals that the narration still has something to teach them (and us). And this is no longer the narration of the practice of Jesus as he was traveling around Palestine in his own lifetime but the narration of Mark at Rome in A.D. 71. For if the disciples seem to have understood nothing until the death of Jesus, the very existence of the text of Mark witnesses the fact that the narration of the practice of Jesus was in fact a message of happiness at the time it was written down.

ABSENCE PERMITS RECOGNITION

What happened, then, between these two periods? What happened is that Jesus was no longer there! The incompleteness with which Mark's Gospel ends indicates that the narration continues, in spite of the fear. On the *road* of the nations, the circle of the counterfield created by Jesus continues to have its tearing and happy effect.

Why? Everything happens as if the presence of the body of Jesus had prevented the disciples from truly recognizing him. The story of the disciples on the way to Emmaus (Luke 24:13–35) is significant. They did not recognize him in the flesh and blood, but only when he undertook the practice of breaking bread and sharing it. Is this not proof that this practice symbolized henceforth the presence of Jesus in the words "This is my body" (Mark 14:22)? Only the *absence* of his body permits recognition of the fact that the messianic practice of sharing brings happiness. As long as he was present, the power and dynamism emanating from him and his practice dazzled—literally fascinated—the crowds and the disciples. When he was absent, his narration *could* finally engage hearers and readers freely in a dialectic between their own practices and his subversive force. This *work* of reading Mark's Gospel bears happiness within itself. This is the emptiness or blank that the Gospel is involved in probing as it attempts to indi-

cate the location of that emptiness. It was necessary for Jesus'
place to be empty so that his ministry might finally have significance. It was necessary for the "Signified One" *par excellence*—
he whose title designated him with so much (or even too much)
evidence as Jesus the Messiah—to disappear in order that the
narrative might finally deliver its good message or gospel.

In this sense the question posed by Mark—Who is Jesus?—is
left for all readers to answer themselves. Mark does not have an
ending; it is not a closed narrative. It loses itself in all the other
narrations of the world in order to better introduce among them
the tearing and the happiness whose shape it subtly outlines.

Chapter 14

The Life and Death Combat

What current editions of the Bible call "the passion and resurrection of Jesus" constitutes in fact a very special grand sequence which we must study separately. It begins at Mark 14:32, and it closes (without a closing) at 16:8. (We have already noted that 16:9–20 is a later addition.)

This sequence is a carefully constructed and developed narrative in which the indications of the author's intervention are especially numerous and obvious. They include the proper names for places: Gethsemane (14:32), Golgotha (15:22); the translation of terms for Roman readers: *abba* = father (14:36), palace interior = praetorium (15:16), Golgotha = place of the skull, *eloi* = my God (15:34), Parasceve or Preparation Day = evening before the Sabbath; personal remarks: "they witnessed falsely" (14:56), "but even on this point their evidence did not agree" (14:59), "for he knew it was out of malice . . ." (15:10). There are also references to personages doubtless known in Rome: "the father of Alexander and Rufus" (see Rom. 16:13); chronological notations: "the third hour" (15:25), "the sixth hour" (15:33), "the ninth hour" (15:34). All of that gives the very strong impression that we have to do here with a carefully worked out text, where nothing has been left to chance. It is, in a way, the chief handiwork of Mark—his highlight as a writer, his summit.

DOUBLE PROLOGUE: TEMPTATION AND ARREST

This narrative within the narrative begins by a kind of *double prologue:* the temptation (14:32–42) and the arrest (14:43–52).

The scene of the temptation is violently marked with the sadness and anguish of Jesus and the passivity and sleep of the three disciples, Peter, James, and John, who were the first to be called (1:16, 19) and the first witnesses of his powerful practice (1:29). Built in three stages that dramatize the situation, the text insists on the hesitation of Jesus on what strategy to adopt. He is "tempted" to choose armed resistance—Zealotism—which he has always refused but which here would be the only adequate reply to the aggression he expects. The aggression begins "while he was still speaking" (14:43), and his decision is made. His body, which has been the source of a powerful and liberating ministry on the side of life, will stand alone against the weapons of the repressive power on the side of death.

The arrest underlines this contrast. On one side are arms, swords, and clubs, the signifiers of the power of the chief priests, scribes, and elders. On the other side is Jesus alone. And the intense emotion that flows from this scene comes especially from the tragic sobriety with which the powerful body of Jesus is reduced to powerlessness, "arrested" in its life-bearing dynamism, in its giving of happiness. The *kiss* of Judas symbolizes this *coup de force*. The sign of friendship becomes the sign of betrayal; it marks for death this body which formerly one only had to touch to be made whole. The abandonment and flight of the disciples accentuates the solitude of the unarmed body, to which the nudity of the young man who ran away in the night (14:52) is like an echo.

Henceforth, the body of Jesus, which has been neutralized by the powerful, will be "led" by their will into the murderous circles of their domination.

THE TWO DEADLY CIRCLES

In fact, the central scene of the sequence is built around two *circles* where the game of *life* and of *death* is played out, as in a theater within the narrative.

The first circle is made by the Sanhedrin assembled around Jesus (14:53–65). In 14:66–67 we find a lesser circle in which a symmetrically balanced scene is played. The symbolical Jewish field is represented here by its quintessence—"the chief priests, elders, and doctors of the law"—gathered to officiate at the ritual murder designed to conjure away the threatening violence.

Once again it is impossible to read this scene at the level of the signified. This "trial" is really not a trial because Mark takes care to indicate that these are false witnesses. Therefore, the ceremony is something other than what it appears. In fact, it is the sacrificial liturgy of the system of purity, which is going to apply the purifying violence to the scapegoat. But the victim is not chosen arbitrarily (see John 10:50: "It is more to your interest that one man should die for the people"). It is the body of Jesus who, as Mark has just shown, is about to "destroy the Temple and replace it." Thus the false witnesses of this false trial reveal, in spite of themselves, the reality of the situation.

The second circle, which overlaps the first, is that of the Roman power, represented by Pilate (15:1–15). Here the "theater" set up by Mark shows in a perfectly clear manner the social formation: the Jewish sub-Asiatic system integrated into the Roman imperial system. The body of Jesus, entirely silent (except for his reply "The words are yours" (15:2), which only acknowledges the situation) is "brought and delivered" like a piece of merchandise to the functionary of the great commercial system that exploited to death the world of that time. Here, also, we must not be taken in by the signified. In fact, there was no real trial, and this legal system of which the Romans were so proud (see Acts 25:16: "It is not Roman practice to hand over any accused man before he is confronted with his accusers and given an opportunity of answering the charge"), this system of justice was obviously in the service of the ruling class. Therefore, Pilate does not seek to know if Jesus is guilty of some violation. What interests him is to maintain the power of Caesar in Palestine, that is to say, not to stir up the crowd against himself. (Apparently Pilate did not always succeed in this effort because the emperor finally relieved him of his powers.) Pilate's problem is to evaluate the danger represented respectively by Jesus (accused of wanting to be "king of the Jews," a Zealot term), and by Barabbas (a Zealot leader arrested during an insurrection that must have taken place at the time Jesus entered Jerusalem).[1] A relationship of forces is operating. Pilate seems persuaded that Jesus is less dangerous than Barabbas, but the Jewish puppet rulers believe the contrary. It is therefore the crowd that decides. But their sympathies go to the more Zealot of the two and, furthermore, they depend economically (in the final instance!) on the Temple directed by the chief priests. The crowd leans, therefore, toward their side. Jesus is very much alone before all these forces that have an interest in having him killed. Thus the circles of power close about him fatally.

But in a supertheatrical effect Mark insists on the extraordinary reversal that has just occurred. Two little scenes, each of them linking the two circles, constitute a lesser drama within the greater one.[2] Lines 14:61–65 set forth the solemn or "theatrical" interrogation of the high priest: "Are you the Messiah, the son of the Blessed One?" Jesus—arrested, bound, visibly reduced to powerlessness—replies no less solemnly: "I am; and you will see the Son of Man seated at the right hand of God and coming with the clouds of heaven." The contrast between the situation of the accused and his response would be more than surprising if it did not have as its precise purpose to lift up the relationship, the connecting link between the narration of his messianic practice and the eschatological narration yet to come.

Thus, in the face of the death threat hanging over his life, Jesus places his hope in the victory of life over death. And it is this crazy hope that tears once more a symbolic Jewish tissue, in this case the robes of the high priest. But this provocation arouses immediately the brutal repression of the murderous power: "and the High Priest's men set upon him with blows."

Parallel to this, lines 15:16–20 set up a horrible puppet show. The body of Jesus, manipulated by the underlings, is vested step by step with the signifiers of imperial power (the purple, crown, and scepter, and the bowing in homage) which in a dramatic parody signify inversely the total powerlessness of this body which will be put to death.

Now comes the supreme derision to underline the complete failure of Jesus' practice. He is ostensibly designated as a Zealot. In fact, crucifixion is the death the Romans reserved for fugitives, slaves, and Zealots.[3] (We have seen that they were often the same individuals.) The inscription of the motive for the condemnation "King of the Jews" (15:26) is one typically associated with Zealots. Finally, the two others crucified with him are called thieves or terrorists (15:27), the name the established powers have always given to rebel insurgents.

THE VICTORY OF DEATH

The execution is also represented in an obviously theatrical manner (15:20–37). The place is designated by its local name, especially translated for Roman readers: Golgotha, which means "place of a skull." The indication of time is no less precise: at the third hour. All the social groups which have had a role in the narration are called together around the cross to interpret the final scene: the crowd of passersby; the high priests with the scribes; and, on the Roman side, the soldiers who execute their task without forgetting to divide up the clothes of the condemned. But the disciples are absent; Jesus is decidedly all alone. The accent is put on the derision: "the passersby hurled abuse at him"; "the chief priests and lawyers jested with one another"; "even those who were crucified with him taunted him." The narration intensifies its own inversion. The powerful body of Jesus has been reduced to nothing.

And the sequence tragically completes itself by an immense cry of despair, "My God, my God, why hast thou forsaken me?" which was written in the original Aramaic and translated into Greek. This cry is set in counterpoint with a sarcastic expression: "Let us see if Elijah will come to take him down." And immediately this is followed by the last gasp of expiration—the atrocious convulsions of life against the frightful violence of death.

But hardly has death come to carry off the victory than the text immediately records the shock waves that upset again the course of the narration: "the curtain of the temple was torn in two from top to bottom." Like a dying beast that ejects its own poison, the old symbolic Jewish tissue did not resist this fatal blow. On the other hand and at the same time, a Roman centurion, who "saw how he died," proclaims: "Truly this man was a son of God." It is thus toward the pagans that the narration has already turned. Finally, "a number of women were also present, watching from a distance" (15:40); it is noted that they "had all followed him . . . in Galilee . . . and had come up to Jerusalem with him." Therefore by implication the disciples are held in reserve by the narrative at this point for other adventures to come.

Nevertheless, the body of Jesus was enclosed in a tomb, but only after the Roman administration had officially registered his death. And a stone closed definitively (?) this story. The powers of death were able to attend to their business with tranquillity. The narration of the practice of Jesus was buried.

DEATH DOES NOT STOP THE NARRATION

And yet . . . the women were still there (15:47), looking as if they were expecting something. And suddenly the narration takes off again! All the codes are rewoven. The chronological indicators pile up in the light of a new dawn: "When the Sabbath was over . . . very early on the Sunday morning, just after sunrise" (16:1–2). The look of the women (16:4–6) emphasized their desire to read this incredible event, which began to unfold before their eyes. The "youth sitting on the right-hand side, wearing a white robe" symbolized the power of the body at work once more. And his words rewove the narration of the practice of Jesus from the beginning ("the man of Nazareth"), through his death ("the one who was crucified"), and from thence in the direction of the pagans ("He is going on before you into Galilee . . .").

Thus death has not had the last word and could not stop the narration. Death had barely laid the body of Jesus to rest in the earth when it was "raised again" (16:6). In the same way at his call were "raised up"—the same word was used—the mother-in-law of Simon (1:31), the paralytic (2:12), the man with the withered hand (3:3), the daughter of Jairus (5:41), the epileptic child (9:27), and the blind man of Jericho (10:49).

We note that there is no question in the text of "resurrection." Mark's Gospel *does not say* that Jesus was raised—nor much less how. Mark has it *announced* by the young man in white. This signifies that henceforth the absent body of Jesus is going to continue to be a factor of power through the narration of his practice as continued by his disciples in the midst of the pagans.

And that is what frightened the women. Jesus was no longer there, and they did not see him again. There is nothing to tell except that this was declared to them: "He is going on before you into Galilee; there you will see him as he told you." With this promise alone, unbelievable as it may be, they must set out on the highways of the world. Now and for always the narration of the practice of Jesus was confided to those who follow him on the road of sharing and reciprocity among living bodies.

Chapter 15

Powerlessness Gives Rise
to Theology

In our readings of Mark, we have left along the way four sections to which we must now return. These are the three announcements of the Passion (8:31–33; 9:30–32; 10:32–34) and the Transfiguration (9:2–3).

MYTHOLOGY AND IDEOLOGY

Right away, we discover *discourses*—the verbs are in the future tense. But on the other hand, the apocalyptic figure of the "Son of Man" and, in the Transfiguration scene, the mountain, Moses, Elijah, the cloud, and the heavenly voice are sure signs of a *mythological* code. We thus have to do with a very particular ensemble that closely resembles the eschatological discourse of chapter 13.

Obviously, these mythological discourses are in flagrant contradiction with the narrative logic of the narration, which relies on contingencies. The foreknowledge that Mark suddenly bestows on Jesus negates the condition—Jesus' lack of foreknowledge—that determines all the narration of his practice. This brutal introduction of predetermination in the midst of risk or chance shows a textual adjustment of the author, who felt the need to "remythologize" his text.

Why?

The conditions of the production of Mark's Gospel can clarify

111

this process. Let us remember *the situation of Christians* in Rome in A.D. 71.

On the *economic* level, the majority of them were recruited among the levels of the population that lived in poverty. But especially because of slavery there was no technological progress leading to a change in the productive forces.[1] The relationships of production were therefore blocked. This was translated on the *political* level into total powerlessness in the face of the Roman Empire supported by the army. There was, therefore, no hope in that direction.

In these conditions we have seen that, on the *ideological* level, the poor as well as the rich, and especially nobles who had been deprived of power, found refuge in sects imported from the East, which historians call "religions of salvation."

Thus the ideological factor was stressed over the economic and political factors. The messianic practice of Jesus was to find itself ideologized. This means that it was to be taken up into a theocentric discourse, which is called theology.

THE THREE STAGES OF THE NARRATION

To understand how this process functioned on the level of the textual work of Mark, we shall take up again the structure of the parables of chapter 4: the soils, the sower, and the mustard seed. We recall that they unfolded in three steps: the sowings, the growth, and the harvest.

These three stages symbolized fairly well the movement of the narration of the practice of Jesus. This movement was sown in Palestine and among all the nations; it grew during the first Christian generation; and the eschatological return of Jesus should bring on its harvest. This is the very structure we have observed for the whole of Mark's Gospel.

We find this confirmed in a series of passages that are distinguished by the following introductory formula: "Truly, I say to you. . . ." When closely examined, they are all seen to be set up in the three stages we have just indicated. The examples follow:

—First stage: there will be no sign for this generation (8:12); Mount Zion will be cast into the sea or abyss (11:22), an allusion to the fall of Jerusalem in A.D. 70.

—Second stage, that of the first Christian generation: the widow's mite (12:43), a symbol of the new economy of sharing; the anointing at Bethany (14:9), a foretelling of the absence of the body of Jesus and the presence of the "poor with you always"; "one of you will betray me" (14:18), an allusion through Judas to the betrayals during the persecutions of Nero; "You will have disowned me" (14:30), the same meaning, except that Peter denied Jesus in words whereas Judas betrayed him in action, which will be a grid for reading the problem of the *lapsi*—Christians who "fell from grace" during the persecutions.

—Third stage, the return of Jesus and the coming of the kingdom of God: the last judgment (3:28); the coming of the kingdom of God before the death of this generation (9:1); conditions of reward and punishment on Jesus' return (9:41); one must enter the kingdom as a little child (10:15); this generation will not pass away before all of this—the end of the world—happens (13:30); the kingdom of God (14:25).

Finally, one of these passages with "Truly, I say to you" sums up simultaneously the three stages: "There is no one who gives up home . . . (1st stage); who will not receive in this age . . . (2nd stage); . . . and in the age to come . . . (3rd stage) (10:29–31).

This shows the textual work by which Mark articulates explicitly the narration of Jesus on one hand with the ecclesial narrations of the first generation of Christians, and on the other hand with the last eschatological narration, that is, the coming of the kingdom of God.

THEOLOGY AND PREDESTINATION

What happened between the first and second stages? There was the propagation of the narration of Jesus outside Judea among the pagan nations. It was the exodus announced by the statement: "He will go before you into Galilee." And the Acts of the Apostles shows that this work was essentially the doing of Paul, who at the same time began to structure in his epistles the first theological discourse. Furthermore, between the second and third stages there was the writing of Mark, who, as we have seen, based the proximity of the last narration on the fact that the ruin of Jerusalem fulfilled the promises of Jesus.

We therefore have in this the spring of the mechanism that operated to ideologize the narration of Jesus' practice.

In fact, in the stage of propagation of the narrative among the pagans, Paul began to make of Jesus the Messiah, "the Lord Jesus Christ" (1 Thess. 1:1).[2] The signifier Messiah, which plays an essential role in the narration of the practice of Jesus, became the fetish or ghostlike double with which readers henceforth can identify themselves, losing thereby their active role in the reading and analysis of their own narrations by the grid of the narration of Jesus. The proof is that the word *Christ* has lost its true meaning—*Messiah*—and has become, in effect, a fetish in the Marxist sense of the word.

During the earlier stage, while Mark's Gospel was being written, this process continued primarily through the work of re-mythologizing a narration whose mythological code already held a certain importance. This narration, however, was counterbalanced right after its prologue by the logic of narrating itself. The mythological discourses (chapter 13, the "Truly, I say unto you" passages, and the announcing of the Passion) constitute for us the traces of this textual work.[3]

Finally, when the first Christian generation disappeared before the coming of the kingdom of God, a final change occurred. This is shown through the editing of the three other Gospels. The contingency of the narration was subordinated to the predestination of the discourse. In these Gospels the death and resurrection of Jesus will be programmed theologically. This will culminate in John's Gospel with the incarnation of the Word of God.

Mark only represents a stage in this process of theologization, which will result in constituting Christianity as the practice of a dominant ideology. One of the clearest indicators of this was the progressive transformation through theology of the murder of Jesus into a predestined sacrificial death in the system-of-purity sense, that is, as blood shed for the remission of sins (Matt. 26:28).

Thus by a movement similar to that of the priests after the Exile who fenced in the popular narrations and lifted them up as Law, the narration of the practice of Jesus was cut off from the ecclesial narrations and became the gospel, the word of God, and the holy scripture. And it is not surprising after this to see that this theo-

logical work—the fruit of economic and political powerlessness—coincided with the appearance in the organization of the
Christian communities of priests and bishops. By a curious return
or detour, the *path* of following Jesus is thus brought back full
circle, closed up from then on, and concerned with its unity and
institutionalization.

More than one reader will perhaps think: Did it require so many
arguments to arrive simply at the famous expression of Loisy:
"Jesus announced the kingdom, and it was the Church that
came. . ."?[4]

It seems to us, however, that our analysis brings out the role of
the conditions of production in this process of theologization.
That could well have important consequences.

First of all, let us consider Mark. At least we have perceived
with how much textual work he demythologized and remytholo-
gized. We note in passing that this absolutely prohibits our trying
to imagine to what exact "signified individual" he was referring,
or what might have been in reality the practice of Jesus. We only
know the text or the texts. Twenty centuries later we must be satisfied with that.

On the other hand, it could be interesting to think that the
economic and political conditions of today undoubtedly render
possible another functioning of the reading of this text which
would no longer overemphasize the ideological. And this is the
reason for our essay on materialist approaches!

This is also the reason for the considerations to which we shall
dedicate our next chapters.

Chapter 16

To Have Faith or to Practice Faith, Hope, and Love

We have not finished with Mark.

In nine chapters we have attempted materialist approaches. Is it worth the trouble? What interest can this kind of reading have today? Are there not more urgent tasks?

It is indispensable that these questions be posed and debated among all persons—Christians or non-Christians—who sense the importance of these issues. We emphasize this because we have the feeling that essays like Fernando Belo's are able to modify the manner in which up to now the Marxist tradition has looked upon Christianity—exclusively as an ideology and therefore essentially as a superstructure. We refer again to the following statement by Engels: "The economic structure of society always forms the real base from which, in the last analysis, is to be explained the whole superstructure of legal and political institutions, as well as of the religious, philosophical, and other conceptions of every historical period."[1]

Admittedly, the famous phrase "in the last analysis" introduces the principle of a dialectic among the three levels, but nearly all Marxists, including Gramsci, hardly took account of it in their analyses of the Christian religion. In the first place, that is due obviously to the fact of the ideologization which at an early date rapidly and radically transformed Christian practice into Christian religion and then transformed Christian religion into Christianity. But perhaps it was also due to an insufficiently materialist reading of the Christian texts.

For we have observed at length that the narration of the practice of Jesus according to Mark developed at the economic, political, and ideological levels.

It is even possible to notice that each level was underlined, as it were, in Mark's Gospel by an indication stemming from a particular function of the human body:

1:41 Jesus stretched out his *hand*, touched him;

1:31 He came forward, took her by the *hand*, and helped her to her feet.

3:10 For he cured so many that sick people of all kinds came crowding in upon him to *touch* him.

5:23 I beg you to come and lay your *hands* on her to cure her and save her life.

5:28 If I *touch* even his clothes, I shall be cured.

5:41 Then, taking hold of her *hand*, he said to her, "Get up, my child."

6:6 He put his *hands* on a few sick people and healed them.

6:13 They drove out many devils, and many sick people they *anointed* with oil and cured.

7:33 He took the man aside, away from the crowd, put his *fingers* into his ears, spat, and *touched* his tongue.

8:22 There the people brought a blind man to Jesus and begged him to *touch* him.

8:23 Then he spat on his eyes, laid his *hands* upon him, and asked whether he could see anything.

8:25 Jesus laid his *hands* on his eyes again.

This work of the hands, which transforms bodies and returns them to life—to work, to speaking, and to love—consists, we might say, of a practice operating at the *economic* level. This appears to be corroborated by the Pharisees in 3:2—to heal is a *work* and thus is prohibited on the Sabbath.

TRAVELING ABOUT: MOVEMENT OF THE FEET

The verbs "to go," "to come," "to leave," "to enter," and "to go out" obviously and very frequently refer to the movement of the feet. We have already noted the importance of the image of the road and of walking after or following Jesus. Other texts might be cited, for example:

1:16   Jesus was *walking* by the shore of the Sea of Galilee.
2:23   One Sabbath he was *going through* the corn fields.
4:1   He had to *get into* a boat on the lake.
6:7   On one of his teaching *journeys* round the vil-
        lages. . . .
6:9   They might *wear sandals*, but not a second coat.
10:32   Going up to Jerusalem, Jesus *leading* the way. . . .
10:50   At that he threw off his cloak, *sprang up*, and came to
        Jesus.

We have seen in chapter 11 that these journeys were not only geographical but strategic and symbolic. The practice of Jesus designated a counterfield where relationships reigned that were reciprocal rather than dominating, that were opposed to the Jewish symbolic field centered on the Temple and governed by the chief priests. The relation of forces was to occur in the end in favor of the latter, and the road of the narration was to pass through the murder of Jesus. It was a question, therefore, of the *political* level.

THE EYES AND EARS

The eyes and ears refer to what we have called the analytical code, which serves to identify the practices of the readings of different personages. In addition to innumerable expressions like "he beheld" and "they saw," we especially find passages like these:

2:5   *Seeing* their faith.
3:1   They were *watching* to *see* whether Jesus would cure
        him on the Sabbath, so that they could bring a
        charge against him.
4:4   If you have *ears* to hear, then hear.
6:14   Now King Herod *heard* of it.
6:38   Go and *see*.

7:14   *Listen* to me, all of you, and understand this.

7:35   With that his *ears* were opened.

7:37   They said, "He even makes the deaf *hear* and the dumb speak.

8:15   Be on your *guard* against the leaven of the Pharisees and the leaven of Herod.

8:18   Are your minds closed? You have *eyes*; can you not see? You have *ears*; can you not hear?

10:21   Jesus *looked* straight at him.

10:49   The blind man answered: "I want my sight back."

12:28   Then one of the lawyers, who had been *listening* to these discussions and had *noted* how well he answered, came forward.

13:7   When you *hear* the noise of battle near at hand and the news of battles far away, do not be alarmed.

13:14   But when you *see* "the abomination of desolation" usurping a place which is not his.

13:26   Then they will *see* the Son of Man coming in the clouds with great power and glory.

14:64   You have *heard* the blasphemy. What is your opinion?

15:4   You *see* how many charges they are bringing against you.

15:33   At midday a *darkness* fell over the whole land.

15:39   The centurion who was standing opposite him *saw* how he died.

15:40, 47   *Watching* from a distance.

16:2   Just after *sunrise*   [in contrast with the preceding darkness]

16:4   When they *looked up* and *saw* that the stone, huge as it was, had been rolled back already.

16:7   You will *see* him there, as he told you.

In studying the parable of the soils (where "hearing" occurs frequently), we learned that the practices of readings are determined by the place or social space where their authors are located. Only those who leave the circle of the dominating class become disciples. In short, Mark is a sort of vast lesson in the reading of the narration of the practice of Jesus (therefore at the *ideological* level). But Mark is also a lesson for a materialist reading because this lesson is always articulated at the three levels of social practice.

REREADING THE GOSPEL

If these words had not been so misused, we might call *love* the economic practice of hands, *hope* the political practice of feet, and *faith* the ideological practice of eyes and ears. We would say then that it is this triple practice which Mark designates as messianic and which is read by its readers as Christian.

Consequently, our problem is no longer to ask ourselves "Do I have faith?" but "What is our practice on these three levels?" and "What relation does our faith have with the narration of the practice of Jesus?"

Now if it is relatively easy to take stock of our present practices, we still have to specify why and how we think we can relate them to texts two thousand years old. We repeat that it is a question of relating to *texts*. In fact, as we have seen, it is not directly Jesus whom we reach but rather *writings* which we read. Mark does not transmit a "signified one"—the message of Jesus—but gives us a certain work on the "signifiers"—words and sentences joined in a certain order—which bear all the way to us a shock wave and a movement that provoked this work, that run throughout it, and that reach us today.

We agree with the beautiful definition of Michel de Certeau:

> I call *writing* the tracing of a desire in the system of a language (professional, political, scientific, and not only literary) and therefore the implanting in a body (a body of law, a social body, the body of a language) of a movement which alters it.[2]

The tracing which Mark has worked into the system of a written language points to such implanting—the altering movement brought about by Jesus implanted in the social body of Palestine of the first century. It is this movement we have called "tearing." In effect, it means recentering desire from the value of exchange to the value of use; establishing here and there, more and more, an economy of sharing and an antiauthoritarian and non-dominating politics; permitting each one to achieve readings of his or her practice and understanding that of others; in brief, liberating bodies (heart, spirit, and flesh) beginning with one's own. This is the life to which this text calls us and to which it witnesses that death cannot win out.

In this sense, Mark continues to be today a good news and a fortunate message. But it is on the condition that we seize Mark's Gospel from those who have never hesitated to enclose it, to make of it a Law, a heavy burden (Matt. 23:4). A materialist reading is therefore always inseparable from a certain liberating economic and political practice. It is because we struggle to overcome the society of classes and the exploitation of human beings that we want to reread again the texts in which a desire is born that was strong enough to face death.

Chapter 17

Insurrection and Resurrection

The text of Mark witnesses essentially to this power of life which even death cannot destroy.

It is not surprising, therefore, that the renown of the practice of Jesus (1:28) hangs principally on the fact that he raised bodies prostrated by fever, sickness, and death.

Let us look at these narrations of miracles a little. A modern tendency of exegesis, as illustrated by Bultmann, has undertaken to demythologize them.[1] But this school remains in the framework of idealist logocentrism, and its rationalist a priori against the possibility of miracles leads it to neglect the materialness of the narrative text and to lift up in the Gospels the teaching, the logia—the so-called authentic words of Jesus, in short, the discourse—to the detriment of the narration of the practice articulated at the three levels. From what we have seen it is rather like reading Mark backwards.

This approach therefore prevents any kind of understanding of the confrontation of life and death that culminates in the murder of Jesus and in the affirmation: "He is risen!"

THE POWER THAT RAISES UP THE LIVING . . . AND THE DEAD

It will be remembered, in fact, that the announcement of the young man in white to the women was linked, by him, to the whole narration of the practice of Jesus:

You are looking for Jesus of *Nazareth*, who was *crucified*. He has risen; he is not here; look, there is the place where they *laid* him. But go and give this message to his disciples and Peter: "He will go before you into *Galilee* and you will see him there, *as he told you*" [16:6–7].

That really constitutes a brief résumé of the whole narration of Mark. What is meant by the resurrection makes no sense except in relation to all the rest.

We can verify this with a particular scene, 12:18–27. In reply to a leading question of the Sadducees (who did not believe in the resurrection of the body, a late belief imported from Persia), Jesus declared:

You are mistaken, and surely this is the reason: you do not know either the scriptures or the power of God. When they rise from the dead, men and women do not marry; they are like angels in heaven. Now about the resurrection of the dead, have you never read in the Book of Moses, in the story of the burning bush, how God spoke to him and said, "I am the God of Abraham, the God of Isaac, and the God of Jacob"? God is not God of the dead but of the living. You are greatly mistaken.

What does this mean? To affirm the resurrection of the dead, Jesus reopened the scriptures enclosed by the priestly caste. He read his own narrative as a continuation of and in the same movement as those of Moses, Jacob, Isaac, and Abraham. For him it was the same power of God which was at work in each of them and to which the scriptures witnessed. Consequently, it was the same thing not to know how to read the ancient narratives and to refuse to read those of Jesus. The same blindness, tied to the positions of classes, closed the eyes and ears of his adversaries. For them, in fact, God was a God of the dead; the promises made to Abraham and others had lapsed; the system of the clean and the unclean led to death, and the Temple, the center of this field, was doomed to ruin. After A.D. 70 this affirmation was to resound powerfully in the ears of the readers of Mark.

Thus the God of the living was hailed by Jesus as the God whose power animated Jesus' practice and who, after raising up a descendant of the aged Abraham and raising up a people from slavery with Moses, would be able to raise up other bodies again.[2] Mark's narration therefore links the totality of the practice of Jesus to the resurrection by referring that practice to the great founding narratives and by establishing that Jesus' power was attributed to God. (Remember that the word *resurrection* does not appear in Mark; it was an early formula of a creed and was taken up by Paul in Romans 1:4 and elsewhere). The narrative of Mark was not closed, as we have noted. It remained open to the narration of the practices of its readers, new and powerful practices that liberate bodies and thus also stem from the God of the living.

This is to say again that the problem of God and the problem of the resurrection have no meaning aside from the triple practice of faith, hope, and love, as analyzed in the preceding chapter. Or, to speak positively, it is only at the heart of a practice aiming at the *in-surrection* of bodies that the question can be posed validly of their *re-surrection*.

THE RESURRECTION: AN OPEN QUESTION

But these observations do not exhaust the question. We are more aware of this when we examine more closely the mythological code of Mark. We remember that it functions especially for the prologue and for the three announcements of the passion and resurrection as well as for the Transfiguration and the eschatological discourses of chapter 13.

Concerning the prologue, we had noticed that the mythological code permits the unfolding of the narrative by carving out, in a way, a block of time in the infinity of eternity. For the Transfiguration, what is striking is the relation and opposition made between heaven and earth: "His clothes became dazzling white, with a whiteness no bleacher on earth could equal" (9:3). The dazzling quality indicated by the narrative comes from the brilliance attributed to the mythological heaven. In the three announcements of the passion and resurrection, it is on the mythological code with its figure of the Son of Man that theology was grafted to announce ahead of time the destiny of Jesus. Thus the resurrection of Jesus was situated by Mark both on the level of the narrative and on the mythological level.

This is to say that the resurrection has an ambiguous status, on the borderline between time and nontime, between space and nonspace, at the juncture of the finite and the infinite, there where our earthly narrations break out into another dimension. This must be kept in mind in evaluating the concept of resurrection, halfway between the observable fact (which it is not at all, as we have seen) and the symbolic image (which it is not "only"). It is undoubtedly this very special situation that gives to the resurrection the possibility of serving in Mark in such a way as to overcome death, which is the end of any further narration, and to start up again all the narrations of liberating practices. These practices are linked onto the narration of the messianic practice toward an infinite that is undetermined by any definition. But the resurrection is also joined to the eschatological last narration, which will be that of the kingdom of God.

It is obvious that here the risk is great of falling into theological idealism or science fiction. But we think that we have sufficiently rooted the concept of resurrection in the materialness of the text of Mark and therefore of the narration of the practice of Jesus, so that it cannot escape and start a new alienating discourse.

For the rest, that depends on us and on our present practices. It suffices, but it is also necessary, that our practice of faith, hope, and love be economic and political enough to avoid letting it become ideologized and hypostasized. By "hypostasized" we mean transformed into an abstract substance in the heaven of ideas. Then the *question* of the resurrection, like the *question* of God, would remain an open question—open to the future of our own narrations and of their possible victory over death.

Epilogue

It is not possible to conclude.

First of all, this is because these approaches are far too experimental for us to be able to consider them terminated. Also, other efforts are already being undertaken here and there to carry on the task. Fernando Belo himself had drawn up a first list of research possibilities in the line of his work.[1] And a small study group, associated with the publication *Lettre*, has been assembled.[2] The group has the intention of studying the history of the church from a materialist perspective. In fact, the notion has arisen that the very idea or concept of *a* history of *a* church is in the same category as the idea of *a* Bible, which we criticized in our first chapter. It is a construction every bit as artificial, ideological, and clerical. If people would look more closely, they would see that there has always been, even from the beginning, many different and often opposing Christian practices. This can be observed, for example, in two ways:

—The "canon" of writings, the official and exhaustive list of books recognized as holy scriptures, for a long time has been the object of bitter controversies. What criteria served to accept one text and reject another? Why have we kept the Revelation of John and not that of Baruch? Why the Gospel of Luke and not that of Thomas? It is a fascinating problem, full of consequences for the way in which we read those texts.

—At the same time, the heresy/orthodoxy dichotomy can teach us a great deal about contemporary situations. Who has the power to marginalize, on what authority, and in whose name? When we think of the attitude of the Catholic hierarchy in many areas, we quickly perceive the importance of the question.

But we must go further. Is the church not already an idealist concept that covers, masks, beautifies, and therefore reveals under criticism an extremely diversified reality that is historically situated and always shot through with class struggle?

To recognize this is not to reject the church in the name of the Gospel, but it is to acknowledge what the church has been and what it is. On this matter also in-depth studies should be made, and some are already under way.[3]

Perhaps we should especially try to define more exactly the church we want to help build, if that is our commitment. To distinguish it from the Roman Catholic church, which is hierarchial, clerical, and often oppressive and repressive, and which we no longer want, we should call it *ecclesia*—from the old Greek word meaning "gathering"—a word which Paul attributed right away to the first Christian groups.

The evolution of the use of the word in Paul's letters, furthermore, will clarify for us its significance.[4] First of all, the *ecclesia of God* designated the mother-community of Jerusalem. Then the term was applied to the new communities founded by Paul in Thessalonica, Corinth, and elsewhere. Finally, *ecclesia* became the name of the totality of all the Christian communities, Jerusalem and the others. The first turning point, the movement from the first to the second meaning, was marked by the Council of Jerusalem (Acts 15). Paul and Barnabas there "reported all that God had done through them" (15:4). That is to say, it was the narration of the mighty practice (cf. the power of God mentioned in the preceding chapter) that had been carried on among the pagans that led the apostles to recognize that the same Spirit had been given to Christians coming from paganism as to those coming from Judaism (15:8). The second turning point—that is, from the second to the third meaning—was marked by the fact that Paul collected money in the new ecclesias to bring help to the one in Jerusalem (see notably 1 Cor. 16:1-4). After his arrest in Jerusalem in A.D. 58, writing to the Colossians and Ephesians during his captivity in Rome in A.D. 61-63, Paul used *ecclesia* for the first time in a general sense, as if the economic practice of love had brought about the unity of all the ecclesias.

Can we not deduce from this that *ecclesia* never designates only a gathering but rather the specific practice of these communities articulated at the economic, political, and ideological levels as faith, hope, and love? Our ecclesia would be therefore the place of a messianic practice in the absence of the body of Jesus, which is signified by this very practice.

The ecclesia we want to build is not therefore a building nor a structure nor an institution but a space, a field designated by the practices of life and read through the grid of the narration of the practice of Jesus.

Notes

CHAPTER 1 THE BIBLE AS SCRIPTURE

1. Karl Marx and Friedrich Engels, *The German Ideology,* in Lewis S. Feuer, ed., *Marx and Engels: Basic Writings on Politics and Philosophy* (New York: Anchor Books, 1959), 247.

2. Louis Althusser, *Fox Marx* (New York: Vintage Books, 1970), 166.

3. Marx, *A Contribution to the Critique of Political Economy,* in Feuer, 43.

4. Engels, *Herr Eugen Dühring's Revolution in Science (Anti-Dühring)* (New York: International Publishers, 1972), 32. See also n. 1 to chap. 16 below.

5. "The class which has the means of material production at its disposal has control at the same time over the means of mental production, so that thereby, generally speaking, the ideas of those who lack the means of mental production are subject to it. The ruling ideas are nothing more than the ideal expression of the dominant material relationships, the dominant material relationships grasped as ideas; hence of the relationships which make the one class the ruling one; therefore, the [dominant] ideas [are those] of its [the ruling class's] dominance" (Marx and Engels, *The German Ideology,* in *On Historical Materialism* [New York: International Publishers, 1974], 44).

6. On the antiquity of this fragment of a nomad song, see A. Robert and A. Feuillet, *Introduction à la Bible,* vol. 1 (Paris: Desclée, 1959), 344; Eng. trans., *Introduction to the Old Testament* (New York: Desclée, 1965).

7. On the two traditions, Exodus-flight and Exodus-expulsion, see Roland de Vaux, *Histoire ancienne d'Israël,* vol. 1 (Paris: Gabalda, 1971), 349-58; Eng. trans., *The Early History of Israel* (Philadelphia: Westminster, 1978).

8. Concerning the history of the settlement of Canaan, see de Vaux, *Histoire,* 487–509, 547–98, 616–20.

9. On this period at the beginning of the monarchy in Israel, see P. Garelli and V. Nikiprowetzky, *Le Proche-Orient asiatique, les empires mésopotamiens, Israël,* Nouvelle Clio series, no. 2 (Paris: Presses universitaires de France, 1974), 65–68.

10. "This is, without doubt, the first historical writing of Israel which we find in its original state" (H. Cazelles, ed., *Introduction à la Bible,* rev. ed., vol. 2 [Paris: Desclée, 1973], 287).

11. The three lists that we produce (J, E, and P) are from G. Auzou, *La tradition biblique* (Paris: Orante, 1957), 144, 231. The agreement of the exegetes is far from unanimous on all the details of these lists, but we can use the lists for a beginning.

12. Concerning the entire period between Solomon and the end of the Exile, a good historical résumé is found in Garelli and Nikiprowetzky, 118–211.

13. Concerning the period between the return from the Exile and the end of Hellenism, see A. Lods, *Les prophètes d'Israël et les débuts du judaïsme* (1935; reprint, Paris: Albin Michel, 1969), 179–205.

14. Centre d'études et de recherches marxistes, *Sur les sociétés précapitalistes, textes choisis de Marx, Engels, Lénine* (Paris: Éditions Sociales, 1970); id., *Sur le "mode de production asiatique"* (Paris: Éditions Sociales, 1969).

15. Guy Dhoquois, *Pour l'histoire* (Paris: Anthropos, 1971). To be nuanced by the reading of Moses Finley, *The Ancient Economy* (London: Catto and Windus, 1973).

16. See especially Cazelles. The work furnishes, from a different perspective from ours, of course, generally open explanations.

17. *The Letter of Aristeas,* which was undoubtedly written in the first century B.C., recounts how the Bible (the Septuagint) was translated into Greek at Alexandria in the third century B.C. The letter is in R. H. Charles, ed., *The Apocrypha and Pseudepigrapha of the Old Testament,* vol. 2 (1913; reprint, Oxford: Clarendon Press, 1963) 94–122.

18. For a discussion of the "canon of inspired books" see Robert and Feuillet, vol. 1, *Introduction à la Bible,* pp. 31–57. Robert and Feuillet's text, which dates from 1959, is entirely typical of the position we criticize.

19. Tertullian *De praescriptione hereticorum* 37.

20. Vincent of Lerins *Commentaries* 4, trans. Rudolf E. Morris, in vol. 7 of the Fathers of the Church Series (New York: Fathers of the Church, 1949).

21. To better understand this statement, see chapter 12 and the epilogue in this book.

CHAPTER 2 THE SCRIPTURES BEGIN WITH SOLOMON

1. See n. 10 above and n. f. for 2 Sam. 9 in the *Bible de Jérusalem,* rev. ed. (Paris: Cerf, 1973).

2. See our article in *Promesses* 80 (December 1973): 116–23.

3. "It is enough to say that the style itself suggests a scribe who knew closely the personalities of whom he speaks. He wrote when Solomon was alive" (H. Cazelles, ed., *Introduction à la Bible,* rev. ed., vol. 2 [Paris: Desclée, 1973], 289). This opinion, which is based on the classical methods of internal criticism, thus confirms our analysis.

4. J. P. Faye, *Théorie du récit, introduction aux "Langages totalitaires"* (Paris: Hermann, 1972), 9.

5. Karl Marx, *Capital: A Critique of Political Economy,* trans. Samuel Moore and Edward Aveling, vol. 1 (New York: International Publishers, 1967), 35–83.

6. Jean-Joseph Goux, *Economie et symbolique* (Paris: Seuil, 1973). The chapter entitled "Numismatiques" sums up Marx's explanation of the genesis of the money form and shows that it applies to all forms of exchange.

7. See especially E. Benveniste, *Problèmes de linguistique générale* (Paris: Gallimard, 1966), 21ff.; for a more elementary introduction see J. B. Fages, *Comprendre le structuralisme* (Toulouse: Privat, 1967).

8. Guy Dhoquois, *Pour l'histoire* (Paris: Anthropos, 1971).

9. See Gerhard von Rad, *Théologie de l'Ancien Testament,* vol. 1 (Labor et Fides, 1963), 60. Eng. trans., *Old Testament Theology* (New York: Harper, 1962).

10. This is a little like the gesture of Napoleon having himself crowned by the pope in order to take advantage of the legitimacy of the kings of France.

CHAPTER 3 THE ROYAL COURT OF SOLOMON AND THE J DOCUMENT

1. On the tribe of Judah and its origins, see Roland de Vaux, *Histoire ancienne d'Israël,* vol. 1 (Paris: Gabalda, 1971), 487–510; on conditions in the south see ibid., 163–69; Eng. trans., *The Early History of Israel* (Philadelphia: Westminster, 1978).

2. On the origin of the joining of these different traditions, see ibid., 160–72.

3. See especially, H. Cazelles, ed., *Introduction à la Bible,* rev. ed., vol. 2 (Paris: Desclée, 1973), 241. See also Gerhard von Rad, *Theologie*

de l'Ancien Testament, vol. 1 (Labor et Fides, 1963), 49–50; Eng. trans., *Old Testament Theology* (New York: Harper, 1962). And see de Vaux, *Histoire,* 391.

4. See de Vaux, *Histoire,* 383, 397.

5. See Cazelles, 179.

6. Ibid., 199.

7. Ibid., 197.

CHAPTER 4   THE PROPHETIC MILIEU IN THE NORTH, THE E AND D DOCUMENTS, AND THE SYSTEM OF GIFT

1. A. Caquot, in *Histoire des religions,* Encyclopédie de la Pléiade, vol. 1 (Paris: Gallimard, 1970), 429.

2. On the economic situation of this period, see Salo Wittmayer Baron, *A Social and Religious History of the Jews,* vol. 1 (New York: Columbia University Press, 1952), 67–91.

3. See H. Cazelles, ed., *Introduction à la Bible,* rev. ed., vol. 2 (Paris: Desclée, 1973), 215, which situates the editing of the E document under the reign of Joash of Israel (798–783 B.C.).

4. "Studies in-depth, like those of A. Welch, A. Alt, G. von Rad, now tend to place the Deuteronomist in the northern groups"(Cazelles, 216). But Cazelles places the editing process at Jerusalem immediately after 722 B.C. (p. 233).

CHAPTER 5   THE PRIESTLY CASTE, THE P DOCUMENT, AND THE SYSTEM OF PURITY

1. In 598 B.C., after the first capture of Jerusalem, Nebuchadnezzar "carried off all Jerusalem into exile, all the nobles and all the notables, ten thousand of these were exiled, with all the blacksmiths and metalworkers; only the poorest people in the country were left behind" (2 Kings 24:14). In 587 B.C., at the time of the second capture of the city, "Nebuzaradan, commander of the guard, deported the remainder of the population left behind in the city . . . . The commander of the guard left some of the humbler country people as vineyard workers and plowmen" (2 Kings 25:11-12).

2. On the period of the Exile and the return, see A. Caquot, in *Histoire des religions,* Encyclopédie de la Pléiade, vol. 2 (Paris: Gallimard, 1979), 114–47.

3. Exactly 42,360, if one credits Esdras 2:64.

4. Roger Caillois, *Cases d'un échiquier* (Paris: Gallimard, 1970), 24.

5. See especially Claude Lévi-Strauss, *The Elementary Structures of Kinship,* rev. ed. (Boston: Beacon, 1969).

6. G. Bataille, *L'érotisme* (Paris: Minuit, 1957), 234.

7. Rene Girard, *Violence and the Sacred* (Baltimore: Johns Hopkins, 1977). See also n. 4, chap. 9, above.

8. Girard, article in *Esprit* (November 1973): 532. This entire discussion should be read in light of Girard's article and Andre Simon's "Les masques de la violence," in ibid., 515-27.

9. Is not the same process in operation today? Is not the struggle against the system of classes, against the schools, legal structure, medicine, and class family daily stifled by ideological instruments such as television, radio, newspapers, movies, and advertising, by magical discourses on superstars and headliners, by ritual formulas of sports and news items—those blood sacrifices on the front page?

CHAPTER 6   CLASS STRUGGLE IN FIRST-CENTURY PALESTINE

1. For a brief résumé of this period, see Marcel Simon and Andre Benoit, *Le judaïsme et le christianisme antique,* New Clio series, no. 10 (Paris: Presses Universitaires de France, 1968), 49-54.

2. On the economy of first-century (A.D.) Palestine, see Salo Wittmayer Baron, *A Social and Religious History of the Jews,* vol. 1 (New York: Columbia University Press, 1952), 250-85. See also Joachim Jeremias, *Jérusalem au temps de Jésus* (Paris: Cerf, 1967); Eng., *Jerusalem in the Time of Jesus* (Philadelphia: Fortress, 1969).

3. Baron, 264.

4. Concerning the political aspect, see, among others, Eduard Lohse, *Le milieu du Nouveau Testament* (Paris: Cerf, 1973), 38-55; Eng. trans., *The New Testament Environment* (Nashville: Abingdon, 1976).

5. We deal too rapidly with the wisdom literature. For a more detailed discussion, see H. Cazelles, ed., *Introduction à la Bible,* rev. ed., vol. 2 (Paris: Desclée, 1973), 531-38, 717-32.

6. On the apocalyptic literature, see Lohse, *Le milieu,* 65-88.

7. On the rabbinic literature, see Charles Guignebert, *Le monde juif vers le temps de Jésus* (1935; reprint, Paris: Albin Michel, 1969), 38-43, 79-100; Eng. trans., *The Jewish World in the Time of Jesus* (New York: University Books, 1959).

8. Concerning the scribes, Pharisees, Sadducees, Essenes, and Zealots, see Lohse, *Le milieu,* 89-149; Simon and Benoit, *Le judaïsme,* 58-64; and Guignebert, *Le monde,* 185-230.

9. Oscar Cullmann, *Jésus et les révolutionnaires de son temps* (Paris: Delachaux et Niestlé, 1970), 21-22; Eng. trans., *Jesus and the Revolutionaries* (New York: Harper, 1970). With Cullmann, compare Kurt

Schubert, *Jésus à la lumière du judaïsme du 1er siècle* (Paris: Cerf, 1974), 108–19.

10. The estimate was made in this way: one talent was worth ten thousand drachmas (see Jeremias, *Jérusalem*, 135 n. 71), and a Greek drachma was worth one Roman denarius (ibid., 174 n. 6). Matt. 20:2 indicates that one denarius was the daily wage of a farmworker. If farmworkers in the U. S. recieve minimum wage and work eight hours, they are paid $26.80 per day. We can thus make the following calculation: 17 x 10,000 x 26.80 = $4,556,000.

11. Almost the only source of information on this period is *The Jewish War* by the Jewish historian Flavius Josephus (A.D. 37–100). Concerning the burning of the fiscal archives, see 2.31. For a good résumé of this war, see Martin Noth, Fr. trans., *Histoire d'Israël* (Paris: Payot, 1970), 430–53; Eng. trans., *The History of Israel* (New York: Harper, 1958).

CHAPTER 7   CHRISTIANS AT ROME IN A.D. 71

1. Concerning first-century Rome, see especially E. Albertini, *L'empire romain* (1936; reprint, Paris: Presses Universitaires de France, 1970), 99–170.

2. Aelius Aristides, *Eloge de Rome* (elegy for Rome), cited in L. Homo, *Nouvelle histoire romaine* (Paris: Fayard, 1941), 422.

3. See V. Diakov and S. Kovalev, eds., *Histoire de l'antiquité* (Moscow: Progress, 1962), 759. Compare the opposing interpretation in Moses Finley, *The Ancient Economy* (London: Catto and Windus, 1973); Fr. trans., L'économie antique (Paris: Minuit, 1975), 228, n. 47.

4. As to the beginning, rise, and role of slavery in the Roman Empire, see Diakov and Kovalev, 584–98 and 757–63; see also Guy Dhoquois, *Pour l'histoire* (Paris: Anthropos, 1971), 123–34. A much more cautious source is Finley, *L'économie*, 109–10.

5. Appian *Civil Wars* 2.7.

6. Concerning the burning of Rome, see U. E. Paoli, *Vita romana, la vie quotidienne dans la Rome antique* (Paris: Desclée de Brouwer, 1955), 81–82, n. 12.

7. On the importance of the order of knights, see Jean Gagé, *Les classes sociales dans l'empire romain* (Paris: Payot, 1971). For a different opinion, see Finley, *L'économie,* 60.

8. One might think of the Bank of Indochina, the Bank of Suez, the canons of Le Creusot, or the airplanes of the Dassault Enterprises.

9. On the imperial bureaucracy, see Albertini, 79–85.

10. On the revolt of Civilis and the proclamation of the "ephemeral empire of the Gauls," see Albertini, 107–8; and Tacitus *Histories* 4.12–37, 54–79; 5.14–26.

11. Concerning ideology, see Albertini, 132–70; and Diakov and Kovalev, 763–71. Concerning the Eastern religions and the Roman Empire, see A. Caquot, in *Histoire des religions,* Encyclopédie de la Pléiade, vol. 2 (Paris: Gallimard, 1979), 33–80.

12. Suetonius *Lives of the Twelve Caesars* 25 (Claudius).

13. Tacitus *Annals* 15.44, trans., Arthur Murphy (New York: E. P. Dutton, n.d.).

14. Concerning this list of names, see *Traduction oecuménique de la Bible, Nouveau Testament* (Paris: Cerf-Bergers et Mages, 1973), 487 n.s.

15. On Flavius Clemens, see Albertini, 118; and Suetonius 15 (Domitian).

16. On the confusion of Christianity with Judaism, see Albertini, 166.

17. On the organization of the first groups of Christians, see A. Lemaire, *Les ministères aux origines de l'Eglise* (Paris: Cerf, 1971); and Marcel Simon and Andre Benoit, *Le judaïsme et le christianisme antique,* New Clio series, no. 10 (Paris: Presses Universitaires de France, 1968), 173–86.

18. Papias, Bishop of Hierapolis in Phrygia, is quoted in Eusebius of Caesarea *Ecclesiastic History* 3.15,39.

19. Samuel G. F. Brandon, *The Date of the Markan Gospel* (1961) cited by G. Minette de Tillesse, *Le secret messianique dans l'évangile de Marc* (Paris: Cerf, 1968), 434.

CHAPTER 8   THE NARRATION OF A PRACTICE

1. See *The Jerusalem Bible* as an example.

2. E. Benveniste, *Problèmes de linguistique générale* (Paris: Gallimard, 1966), 241.

3. F. de Saussure established the basis of modern linguistics in *Cours de linguistique générale* (1916; reprint, Paris: Payot, 1972).

4. Jean-Joseph Goux, *Economie et symbolique* (Paris: Seuil, 1973).

5. Ibid., 131.

6. Here is the admirable metaphor: "The text, while it is being made, is like a lace of Valencia that is born before our eyes under the fingers of the lace maker. Each sequence undertaken hangs as a temporarily inactive shuttle that waits while its neighbor works; then its turn comes; the hand picks up the thread and leads it over the drum. As the design fills in, each thread marks its advance with a pin that holds it and is moved little by little. Thus the terms of the sequence: there are *positions* occupied that are then passed by in view of a progressive involvement in the meaning. This process is valuable to the whole text. The totality of the codes, when it is taken up in the work, in the progress of the reading, constitutes a braid (text, tissue, and braid are all the same thing). Each thread and each

code is a voice. These voices, braided together or braiding, form a scripture or writing. When it is alone, the voice does not work or transform anything; it *expresses*. But when the hand comes in to gather and mix the inert threads, there is work; there is transformation" (Roland Barthes, *S/Z* [Paris: Seuil, 1970], 166; Eng. trans., *S/Z* [New York: Hill and Wang, 1974]).

7. Ibid., 11 (page numbers refer to French edition).

8. Ibid., 96.

9. Ibid., 19.

10. Ibid., 20.

CHAPTER 9 AN OPEN NARRATIVE: MYTHOLOGY AND HISTORY

1. Paul Beauchamp, *Création et séparation,* (Paris: Aubier-Montaigne-Cerf, 1969).

2. This is the origin of the title of a brochure published with the collaboration of Fernando Belo by the Jeunesse Étudiante Chrétienne (JEC—a Roman Catholic student movement). Entitled *L'évangile de Marc, un recit ouvert* (1974), the pamphlet is available at the office of JEC (27 rue Linné, Paris 5).

3. "The Gospels are presented as situated at the paroxysm of a crisis that John the Baptist defined as sacrificial and prophetic by taking up again for his own purposes the beginning of Second Isaiah: '*Let every valley be filled in, every mountain and hill be laid low*' (Isa. 40:4). It is the great tragic leveling off, the triumph of reciprocal violence. This is why the mutual recognition of John the Baptist and of Christ—the seal of prophetic and messianic authenticity—was first of all the absence of antagonistic symmetry, the simple and miraculous fact of not succumbing to the vertigo of violence" (Rene Girard, article in *Esprit* (November 1973): 551.

CHAPTER 10 A SUBVERSIVE NARRATIVE

1. For the vine, see Isa. 5:1. For the vine and the fig tree, see Jer. 8:13.

2. We give an analysis of this text in *Promesses* 80 (December 1973): 55–58.

3. Rene Girard, article in *Esprit* (November 1973): 552.

4. According to Girard, humanity is born in a state of indifferentiation: one does not distinguish oneself from an "other." One is fascinated by this double; it is the imitative desire that results in a reciprocal violence that renders all social life impossible. The first human societies therefore invented ways of expelling this violence by projecting it upon a scape-

goat, which became the criminal double of all the others. The real event was repeated ritually in religious sacrifices. The *holy* therefore assures the catharsis of violence because it reproduces symbolically and thereby masks the original collective murder. But for the first time the Gospels unmask the secret mechanism of violence: they show how Jesus was sacrificed as a scapegoat and how, in taking on the violence, he revealed and uprooted the structural matrix of all religion. Thus, "the murderers of Christ acted in vain, or rather they acted in a creative fashion in that they helped Christ inscribe the objective verity of violence in the gospel text. This truth, even if it is unknown and opposed, will slowly make its way, affecting all things like an insidious poison" (ibid., 554).

CHAPTER 11   TOPOLOGY AND STRATEGY

1. For the body of Jesus as the direct object of the verbs "to take," "to take away," "to lead away," see Mark 14:53; 15:1; 16:20.

2. In order to have us feel the hope that is raised by calling to mind this strategy of Jesus in Mark's Gospel, which was especially read at Rome after the persecutions by Nero and after the arrival of the news of the destruction of Jerusalem, it is perhaps not out of order to cite here the last lines of *Electra* by Jean Giraudoux:

The woman Narses. How's it called, when the day begins like today and everything is spoiled, everything is ruined, and yet the air continues to be breathed, and everything is lost, the city burns, the innocent kill each other, but the guilty die in a corner of the day that begins?
Electra. Ask the beggar. He knows.
The beggar. That is a very beautiful name, woman Narses. It is called *dawn*.

CHAPTER 13   THE NARRATION POSES THE QUESTION: WHO IS JESUS

1. See Vladimir Propp, *Morphology of the Folktale* (Austin: University of Texas Press, 1968); see also C. Bremond, "Le message narratif," *Communications* 4, and "La logique des possibles narratifs," *Communications* 8.

2. *Encyclopaedia universalis,* s.v. "psychanalyse."

CHAPTER 14   THE LIFE AND DEATH COMBAT

1. Concerning Barabbas, Mark 15:7 states: "Now a man called Barabbas was then in prison with the rioters who had committed murder

during the uprising." This uprising (with the definite article) refers therefore to an event the text has already mentioned. This can only be the entry
of Jesus into Jerusalem during which the crowd was able to give vent to
its anti-Roman sentiments, thus favoring one of the commando actions
common to the Zealots. There is a confirmation of this in a detail of
translation noted by Georges Crespy in his article in *Lumière et vie* 101,
p. 101. According to W. Vischer, the acclamation "Hosanna in the
highest" does not signify very much if it is translated literally as "save us
in the heavens." Vischer argues that the phrase is a transcription from the
Hebrew *HSNN BMRM,* and he explains that only one letter needs to be
changed to have *hsnn lmrm,* which means "save us from the Romans!"
The phrase would then be a subversive cry of the Zealots, which would
have been clear to the crowd but incomprehensible to the foreign soldiers
(W. Vischer, *Die evangelische Gemeinde Ordnung—Mattheus 16, 13–20,
28* (Zurich: Evangelische Verlag, 1946).

2. We purposely use this theatrical vocabulary in order to underscore
the extraordinary textual work of Mark. And this construction of a play
within a play recalls irresistibly act 3, scene 2 of *Hamlet* in which Shakes-
peare intertwines a secondary play with the primary drama.

3. Concerning the cross as a punishment for fugitive slaves, see V.
Diakov and S. Kovalev, eds., *Histoire de l'antiquité* (Moscow: Progress,
1962), 590; concerning the cross as a punishment for the Zealots, especially during the seige of Jerusalem in A.D. 70, see Flavius Josephus *The
Jewish War* 6.28.

CHAPTER 15   POWERLESSNESS GIVES RISE TO
THEOLOGY

1. On this controversial point, compare the conclusions of A.
Aymard in the epilogue to *Stagnation technique et esclavage:* "Slavery
must not be held as a consequence of the absence of machines. On the
contrary, the absence of machines looks to the historian like a consequence of slavery" (*Stagnation technique et esclavage,* vol. 1 of
L'Histoire générale du travail [Nouvelle librairie de France, 1961–62]).

2. It is obvious that this simple reference cannot really show the importance of the role of Paul. It is hoped that deeper studies will be undertaken on this point.

3. The reference of Jesus to the "Father." The word is used four
times in Mark: "The Son of Man would be ashamed of him, when he
comes in the glory of his Father and of the holy angels" (8:38); "And
when you stand praying, if you have a grievance against anyone, forgive
him so that your Father in heaven can forgive you the wrongs you have

done" (11:25); "But about that day or that hour no one knows, not even the angels in heaven, not even the Son; only the Father" (13:32); " 'Abba, Father,' he said, 'all things are possible to thee; take this cup away from me' " (14:36). The first three sentences are part of sequences whose "mythological" character we have already shown, which underlines this time the presence of heaven and the angels: 8:38 follows immediately the first of the three announcings of the passion: 11:25 is included in one of the passages with "verily, I say unto you"; 13:32 belongs to the eschatological discourse of chapter 13. There remains only the famous "Abba"; Jeremias has shown that this was the name that little children gave to their fathers: papa. He deduces from this that Jesus considered this childlike name as the expression of the unique knowledge of God that the Father had given him and of his full powers as the Son: " 'Abba' is the very voice of Jesus in all its original purity" (Joachim Jeremias, *Paroles de Jésus* [Paris: Cerf, 1967]). According to Marie Boismard, the narration of the Agony in Gethsemane in Mark is a composite sequence, where the "contact with Paul" is manifested. In fact, one finds the word *abba* only two other times in the New Testament: Galatians 4:6 and Romans 8:15. In the latter text, the word comes at the end of a development opposing the "spirit" and the "flesh" (Rom. 8:4–13), precisely as in Mark 14:38–the spirit is willing, but the flesh is weak." Boismard therefore concludes that it is possible to "see here an influence of Paul upon the Markan editing" (*Synopse des quatre Évangiles en Français,* vol. 2 [Paris: Cerf, 1972], 394). This would confirm our hypothesis of a "theologization" or "remythologization" perceptible in the work of writing by Mark.

4. A. Loisy, *L'Evangile et l'Eglise* (Paris, 1902), cited by Hans Küng, L'Eglise, vol. 1 (Paris: Desclée de Brouwer, 1968), 71 n. 1: Eng. trans., *The Church* (London: Burns and Oates, 1967).

CHAPTER 16 TO HAVE FAITH OR TO PRACTICE FAITH, HOPE, AND LOVE

1. Friedrich Engels, *Herr Eugen Dühring's Revolution in Science (Anti-Dühring)* (New York: International Publishers, 1972), 32. To this should be added the many nuances that Engels contributed. For example: "According to the materialist conception of history, the *ultimately* determining element in history is the production and reproduction of real life. More than this neither Marx nor I has ever asserted. Hence if anyone twists this into saying that the economic element is the *only* determining one, he transforms this proposition into a meaningless, abstract, senseless phrase" (Letter to J. Bloch, September 21–22, 1890, in *On Historical*

Materialism [New York: International Publishers, 1974], 294). And also: "Political, juridical, philosophical, religious, literary, artistic, etc., development is based on economic development. But all these react upon each other and also upon the economic basis . . . . There is, rather, interaction on the basis of economic necessity, which *ultimately* always asserts itself" (Letter to B. Borgius, January 25, 1894, in ibid., 307). On these issues see also the remarkable work by M. Harnecker, *Les concepts élémentaires du matérialisme historique* (Brussels: Contradictoires, 1974).

2. M. de Certeau, *Le christianisme éclaté* (Paris: Seuil, 1974), 81.

CHAPTER 17   INSURRECTION AND RESURRECTION

1. Rudolf Bultmann, *Jesus Christ and Mythology* (New York: Charles Scribner's Sons, 1958). See also Paul Tillich's statement: "Bultmann combines radical historical research with a systematic attempt which he calls 'demythologizing.' He means by that that we should liberate the biblical message from the mythological language in which it is expressed so that modern man, who does not share the biblical vision of the world, might accept without intellectual dishonesty the biblical message itself" (Fr. trans., *La naissance de l'esprit moderne et la théologie protestante* [Paris: Cerf, 1972], 288; Eng., *Perspectives on 19th and 20th Century Protestant Theology* [New York: Harper and Row, 1967]).

2. This discussion calls to mind William Hinton's book *Fanshen* (New York: Random House, 1966) which retraces the story of the agrarian revolution in a little village in China. Hinton writes, "To make *fanshen* is literally 'to turn one's body,' it is to rise and to stand up as a free man." What a difference from the idealist and pious usage theology has made of the evangelical term *metanoia,* conversion. . . .

EPILOGUE

1. Consider Fernando Belo's remarks:

There are a number of paths that would have to be followed for further work on a materialist ecclesiology that will handle either the other New Testament texts or the later Christian text.

It would be necessary, for example, to see how the theological discourse will find in the mythological "voice" the idea (in the Greek sense of the term) of a "revealed truth" from heaven, an idea that will ground the whole development of dogmatic orthodoxy. How the so-called Apostles' Creed took shape as a mythologized narrative. How the theological discourse will set itself up as theo-logy, a discourse on God, and replace the powerful ecclesial practice that alone is word and alone can proclaim God. How the mythological code is related to the theology of the interiority of souls, a theology of which modern Christocentrism (faith having as its object the "person of Jesus") is the most recent avatar. How baptism-immersion in water will be reintroduced, which Mark clearly opposes to immersion in the Spirit; and also how the practice of baptizing infants was introduced and made general, thus doing away with the break involved in conversion. How the movement of replacing the temple with the body of J and the latter, in turn, with the practice of bread has been turned completely around: the bread disappears in the "host" (signifier of the signified "body of Christ") that is placed in the tabernacles of the temples-churches, so that the latter finally came to give symbolic orientation to the space of the cities and towns of the Middle Ages. How, finally—last but not least—the subversion of the codes of the social formation by ecclesial practice has been annulled. The ANAL code located this subversiveness on the side of the God of the living, while the god of the dead was located in the field of the satanic and death, so that Satan became the symbolic emblem of the chief equivalents of the SOC: money, Caesar, god of the temple. One of the clearest symbols of the remythologizing work done by the episcopal or ecclesiastical theological discourse will be the annullment of this subversion, for heaven will once again connote the powers of the SOC in which the church has installed itself, and it will instead be subversiveness that is repressed as satanic and infernal, something cursed, in accordance with a semantic that has prevailed down to our own day. In short, it would be necessary to examine how, and by what decisive tranformations, a theocentric religion has been able, more or less with impunity, to appeal for its authority to the "good news of Jesus the Messiah" and even to go so far at times as to murder the "heretics" (*A Materialist Reading of the Gospel of Mark* [Maryknoll, N.Y.: Orbis, 1981], 285–86).

2. In February 1975 the journal *Lettre* devoted a special issue to the work of Belo. The journal is available at "Temps présent" at 68 rue de Babylone, Paris 7.

3. See Jean Guichard, *Eglise, luttes de classes et stratégies politiques* (Paris: Cerf, 1972); and Alfred Durand, *Pour une Eglise partisane* (Paris: Cerf, 1974).

4. See Lucien Cerfaux, *La théologie de l'Eglise suivant saint Paul,* 2nd ed. (Paris: Cerf, 1948).

Scripture Index

Compiled by John Boonstra

OLD TESTAMENT

APOCRYPHA

NEW TESTAMENT